Science Confirms Reconnective Healing

Edited by Dr. Konstantin Korotkov

Science Confirms Reconnective Healing

Edited by Dr. Konstantin Korotkov

This book describes results of different experiments and clinical trials exploring the effects of Reconnective Healing. Experiments during three years demonstrated that sessions of Reconnective Healing had statistically significant positive influence on the functional state, humoral activity, physical condition and reaction to loading for the group of people both immediately and in 10 days after the influence. This signifies long-lasting effect of Reconnective Healing and its significance for people's health and well-being. Reconnective Healing does not invoke a relaxation response in the person, but decreases both sympathetic and parasympathetic stimulation of the autonomic nervous system, as observed when a person is in a state of emotional detachment, inner quiet and heightened awareness of the flow of subtle energy. These physiological responses are compatible with the Reconnective Healing principle of sensing and kinesthetically interacting with energy fields, as well as passively allowing the energy to flow through the body. One special effect of Reconnective Healing is structurization of Space in the auditorium, which affects all people present.

ISBN-13: 978-1467948203

© 2012 Korotkov Konstantin

Science Confirms Reconnective Healing

CONTENTS

1   The New Frequencies of Healing

    Dr. Eric Pearl 4

2   An Experimental Investigation of Some Reconnective Healing Workshops Via a Unique Subtle Energy Detector

    Dr. William Tiller, and Dr. Walter Dibble, Jr...................... 12

3   Baseline Testing of Reconnective Healing Practitioners During Self-Healing

    Dr. Ann Linda Baldwin and Dr. Gary Schwartz.......................... 33

4   Reconnective Healing Electrophotonic Experiments 2008 - 2011

    Dr. Konstantin Korotkov.. 47

5   EPI/GDV Technique.. 49

6   Experimental Results... 54

7   Clinical Studies of the Influence of Reconnective Healing.

    The Influence of the Reconnective Healing on Psycho-Physiological State of Athletes..................................... 96

8   Influence of Reconnective Healing on Human Immune Status and Psycho-Physiological State........................... 123

9   Reconnective Healing Water Study 140

10 Conclusions 148

    References 150

1. THE NEW FREQUENCIES OF HEALING

Dr. Eric Pearl

A new science is emerging that is changing our traditional understanding of health and healing. The latest scientific research is focusing on experiments that seek to quantify the effects of a newly accessible comprehensive spectrum of energy, light and information on human beings. This new healing spectrum is referred to by researchers today as *The Reconnective Healing Spectrum*. Leading the way in this research is an international team of world-renowned scientists including such research luminaries as William Tiller, PhD, Gary Schwartz, PhD, and Konstantin Korotkov, PhD, with their studies of the *Reconnective Healing* frequencies, first discovered by Dr. Eric Pearl. The powerful and profound results of this research are attracting the attention of the best and brightest in the scientific community.

Dr. Tiller, Professor Emeritus, Stanford University, author of eight books, 250 scientific papers and co-star of the film *What The Bleep!?* has been conducting research on how the physical properties of a room or space change as a result of energy healing frequencies entering that room during Reconnective Healing seminars. He conducted his experiment on the *Reconnective Healing* frequencies for the first time at one of The Reconnection's seminars held in Sedona, AZ in 2006, and found the results so extraordinary that he repeated his study of this phenomena three more times over the past couple of years, twice in Los Angeles, CA and once in Tucson, AZ just to be certain that his extraordinary data were accurate. What Dr. Tiller has now shown has the medical research community quite baffled.

He explained that although the energy healing techniques we know of today utilize electromagnetic energy, Reconnective Healing brings us

Science Confirms Reconnective Healing

up *"to a higher level... magnetoelectric energy,"* up to a *"higher dimensional level."* In Reconnective Healing, *"what is happening is that many kinds of energy and light are flowing through the healer and into the healee,"* not just what we were accessing before. In other words, the *Reconnective Healing* frequencies bring healing *"beyond just what has been classically known as energy healing into a broader spectrum of energy, light and information,"* a spectrum that may not have been accessible by us prior to now.

Dr. Pearl explains it like this. We exist in our four-dimensional reality– often represented in quantum physics discussions as a *bubble* – in this huge multi-dimensional universe. And the parameters or walls of our bubble – comprised of height, width, depth and *time* – has been filled to capacity with energy. Yet time is moving *faster.* Not just in a linear fashion, not just in one direction... instead it's moving faster in *all* directions at once. In other words, time is *expanding.* And with this it would appear that our playground, our four-dimensional bubble, too, is expanding. And therefore so is our capacity to receive. Suddenly we're able to receive more. More than we've had access to before. More than just the energy that's been here on the planet and its various subsets – Reiki, Qi Gong, etc. – and the endless offshoots that we've accessed through the myriad energy healing techniques. And with this expanded presence, we can now transcend *technique* completely, evolve beyond the need to move our hands in one direction instead of another, the need to sweep up in the front or down in the back, to see past the illusion of up/down/front/back altogether; to protect ourselves in white, violet or gold flames, to inhale to one count and exhale to another, to touch specific points, intend wavelength collapses, spin chakras clockwise or counterclockwise, to blow out, shake off or spray away "negative" energies.

And light being consciousness, with this expanded access to light comes an expanded consciousness. This allows us to see past negative energy as it has all too often been viewed in the healing world, to recognize that darkness doesn't exist, for if it did, we could sweep it up, place it into a paper bag and put it out with the trash. That instead it's only a place where we have not yet allowed ourselves to shine as the light, and that the fear-based concepts of "evil" and "negative" ("bad") energy in healing, and in the field itself, is simply illusion. In other words, we free ourselves from the *shoulds* and *shouldn'ts* of energy healing techniques, old and new. And when we free ourselves from shoulds and shouldn'ts most anywhere in life, we allow ourselves to become more present, more in the moment, to interact more fully and consciously with life, with the field. We go beyond and access a fuller spectrum of healing simply by interacting with it. A spectrum, a *continuum,* of energy, *light* and *information.*

Let's speak about light and information. Our bodies don't heal the way we were taught. It doesn't heal through chemicals. We heal via frequency, vibration, information, resonance... Pearl believes in what he calls *The One-Cause Theory.* The theory is that the degree to which we fall away from perfect health is the degree to which we've temporarily forgotten that we *are* light. And all we need is to do for self-healing is to remember, to remind ourselves in a way that allows us to return to our natural state of light vibration. And as we vibrate in our optimum state of light, anything denser than that light pretty much has nothing left to hold on to, therefore it falls away, *if appropriate at that point on our life path for it to do so.* Studies prove that what Pearl is describing is accurate.

Specifically in one of those studies, Dr. Tiller's findings demonstrate that this new continuum of healing frequencies impressively and conclusively increases what science calls "excess free thermodynamic energy," something released or produced, to a small degree, with energy healing. Dr. Tiller explained that there was such an increase of excess free thermodynamic energy in the Reconnective Healing seminar room that, if this were simply the energy we find in "energy healing" or energy healing "techniques," the temperature of the room would have had to have increased by at least *300 degrees centigrade* to attain healing results even close to this. With *Reconnective Healing,* while the *actual* room temperature does not change, the amount of energy, light and information *charging* the room does, palpably and dramatically. In Dr. Tiller's words,

> *"As we continued to monitor that space, we found **two days** **later the increase in this effective energy content was huge.** [If we ask] 'What is the effective temperature increase for that normal space, how much must it go up to give the same excess*

Science Confirms Reconnective Healing

energy content as was in Eric's workshop two days after he started?" [The answer is] **"The effective temperature increase for a normal space would have been 300 degrees Centigrade! That is huge."**

These findings are highly significant. In offering insight into how people are changed after learning or interacting with Reconnective Healing, Dr. Tiller continues,

> *"This shift of energy is what allows normal human beings to enter a room and later to walk out with an ability to heal others and themselves, regardless of their background or education."*

In another research study, Dr. Gary Schwartz, along with Drs. Melinda Connor and Ann Baldwin from the Laboratory for Advances in Consciousness and Health at The University of Arizona, focused their research on the people who attend *Reconnective Healing* seminars. Dr. Schwartz and his colleagues conducted their "baseline energy healing" studies both at Dr. Schwarz's lab at the University of Arizona and at Reconnective Healing seminars around the world. These studies measured people's abilities to work with, feel, transmit and receive light and other electromagnetic frequencies before and after they attended the seminar. What they found was, in their own words, "dramatic." Of the more than 100 people who participated in the study, *all* walked out with permanently expanded healing abilities following the seminar, whether they had never studied healing or even if they were masters, master teachers or grandmasters of the various energy healing techniques known today, old or new. Furthermore, Schwartz's multiple studies show that Reconnective Healing practitioners can "produce" a wave, or more specifically a bandwidth of frequency waves that literally affect the DNA of living things in a powerful and healing fashion.

While Dr. Tiller has been measuring the very large field effects that occur at these seminars and Dr. Schwartz has been focusing his research on those who attend those seminars, Dr. Korotokov has studied both field effects and effects on individual seminar attendees. Using cutting-edge imaging methodologies and measurement devices, Dr. Korotkov's research corroborates both Dr. Tiller and Dr.

Science Confirms Reconnective Healing

Schwartz's findings. More specifically, he has measured and documented significant field effects, known as "coherence effects," that occur while the teaching is conducted at the seminar. These coherence effects catapult to yet higher levels whenever a new concept or exercise is introduced into the seminar, documented by significant leaps in both the intensity and size of the seminar room's field. He theorizes these coherence effects might be the conduit allowing attendees to acquire these new abilities and become master healers in just one short seminar weekend.

Additionally, Dr. Korotkov's research demonstrates that simply by sitting in the seminar room itself, the overwhelming majority of attendees undergo substantial health improvements, most of them quite significant. This is further confirmed by the many conclusive reports of healings, physical and otherwise, by the seminar attendees.

How does it work?

In truth, we are still not fully certain how this works. Pearl explains however that being a healer, facilitating healing for others beyond the constraints and limitations of energy healing and its techniques, functions as a field experience. Actually, it's a pretty pure experience. You simply step into the equation with the other person and the universe, and allow yourself to *feel*. Feel, observe, play, notice. And as you allow yourself to do this, you become more aware of the field, your sensations, varying sensations – pushing, pulling, buzzing, vibrating, warmth, coolness, moisture, dryness, even unusual combinations such as hot, cold, wet and dry, all at the same time. And although that may be difficult to imagine, once you feel it, you *know* it.

The funny thing about this is the simplicity of what underlies it. If you distill all these sensations they become essentially one: joy, happiness... *bliss*. And as you experience that bliss, you are, of course, in the field. You vibrate at your optimal level of light. And you are, of course, not in the field alone. You are in the field with everyone, specifically with that person who has your *attention*, because, let's face it, we go where our attention is. And somehow in this interaction, consciously or otherwise, a little "voice" – not necessarily literally – inside that person says, *Hey, I remember this. This is me vibrating healthy. This is me vibrating as light... I think I'll do it again.* And in that remembrance, we begin to vibrate at the optimum level again, vibrate healthily. And anything denser than that light, which includes most health challenges for that person at that point in time, simply falls away. Healing is that simple. And anything – *anything* – more complicated than that is designed to sell you something.

Techniques, steps, directions, procedures, amulets, protective necklaces... This is not what healing is made of. This is not what the field is made of. *The gift is the challenge.* The gift is the demystification of accessing the field and the healing process. The challenge is your willingness to allow it to be demystified.

How do you work with the field? How do you teach this? How do people who leave a Reconnective Healing seminar able to access more clearly and more comprehensively a multidimensional field than they were prior their arrival, or than they were through the various energy healing techniques they have had until now? And how do you teach this in a way that allows people to get it?

You can't really *teach* healing. You can't really *teach* field interaction. Field interaction and healing happen to some degree *anyway*. It's a gift. A part of our existence, our presence, our natural function. And yet there's more. And the *more* comes about simply when we allow ourselves to open our awareness to it. Once we see it, once we feel it, once we allow ourselves to recognize what we feel and see, and once we give ourselves permission to *acknowledge it.* For without acknowledgement, our ability to access it fades, because our willingness to access it fades...

The *more* comes about once we allow ourselves to *listen...* with a different sense. To stop *doing* and, instead, to *become.* To become the observer and the observed. This is where and when the universe often chooses to display its wonder and it's beauty for us. This is the gift. We then see things that are new, that are different, that are real. Very, very real. We experience, then, each session with a sense of newness and discovery because, with each person, it *is* new.

We enter into a place on knowingness, we are invited into the *home* of the healing process. It's a doorway that's opened for us, and, in turn, it allows us to open new doors for others. It's a more conscious and aware interaction with the field, and more rewarding for all involved. It doesn't feed the ego of the doer, instead it gives higher and lasting sustenance to all involved with unparalleled healing results because the nature and form of the healing is determined not by the limited, conscious, educated human mind and the ego of doing, but rather by the intelligence of the field, the intelligence of the Universe, Zero Point Field, the Holy Spirit, God, Love, Spirituality, the Axiatonal Grid—or Akashic Field. Once we get out of our own way and allow ourselves to access this field of spirituality, healing, intelligence and evolution, we allow ourselves to experience *oneness*. And once we truly experience it, we get to find out just how normal that really is.

This is healing of a very different nature than we have been taught to perceive, understand, or even believe or accept. This healing is about an evolutionary process brought into existence through *co-creation* at the highest vibrational interaction with the Universe, at the highest vibrational interaction with the field.

We are all here as one.

We have our own vibration... but we are of the same sound.

We all have the music of life.

The benefits of these powerful frequencies, are not just limited to helping people. Animals can also receive healings. For that matter, studies have also shown that plants also benefit from this work. It seems that these new frequencies can restructure our DNA and help all living things to heal on new and comprehensive levels.

What impact are these and other studies on Reconnective Healing having on the scientific and medical community? Traditional science and medicine can no longer approach health and healing in the same manner as they previously have and remain in step with the rest of the world. New scientific exploration by Drs. Tiller, Schwartz, Korotkov, Baldwin, Blair and others, as well as what is documented in Dr. Pearl's internationally bestselling book, *The Reconnection: Heal Others, Heal Yourself*, are validating the powerful effects that this new spectrum of energy, light and information can have on people. This may not only be showing us a new level of healing, it may also be

Science Confirms Reconnective Healing

opening a doorway to the next level of human evolution, where instantaneous healing and regeneration are simple, everyday facts of life - simple, everyday miracles.

Everyone Can Be a Healer

To date, Eric Pearl and his staff at The Reconnection have trained over 70,000 people how to do this work with practitioners in more than 70 countries. While several thousand of those trained worldwide are medical doctors, nurses, chiropractors and/or master healers, most come from non-healthcare related backgrounds and include engineers, teachers, housewives, high school students, sales personnel, attorneys, government officials, celebrities and even royalty! They come from all walks of life, all age groups, and are able to carry this work forward at the highest levels. And they, and their clients, report healings from all types of conditions, similar to those of Pearl's own patients.

Working with these frequencies is often a life changing experience. During a seminar weekend, you are "immersed" in the frequencies, and often continue to experience the healing vibrations well after the seminar has finished. Once activated by this work, your own healing and evolution continue at its own rate, every day, for the rest of your life.

*You, too, can **learn this work in just one weekend.***

*For more information about **Dr. Eric Pearl** and **The Reconnection**, visit **www.TheReconnection.com***

Science Confirms Reconnective Healing

Dr. William A. Tiller, and Dr. Walter E. Dibble, Jr.

2. An Experimental Investigation of Some Reconnective-Healing Workshops via a Unique Subtle Energy Detector

Introduction

Background

Our last dozen years of experimental and theoretical research in the psychoenergetics science area[1-4] has revealed that there are two uniquely different levels of physical reality and not just our normal, electric charge, atom/molecule level. In nature, these two levels of uniquely different kinds of substance appear to function in either (a) the uncoupled state, where they do not interact with each other on a macroscopic level, or (b) the coupled state where they do partially interact with each other.

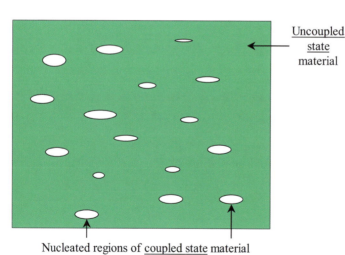

Figure 1. Nucleation and growth of the macroscopic coupled state of physical reality.

Figure 1 provides a schematic illustration of a macroscopic composite of these two uniquely different levels of physical reality. Here, the islands of the coupled state phase nucleate

Science Confirms Reconnective Healing

and grow within the uncoupled state host material (a room in a building, a piece of equipment, a piece of inorganic or organic material, etc.) via the application of a sufficiently strong field of human intention. If that intention field weakens, the size and number of the islands slowly shrink; when that intention field strengthens, the size of the islands slowly grow and the properties of the composite change according to the specific intention utilized in the experiment[1-4]. In our past experiments[1-4], a specific intention was mentally/emotionally embedded into a simple electronic circuit by a small group of people acting from a deep meditative state of consciousness. A small plastic box containing this intention-host circuit was shipped to the experimental site where measuring equipment was continuously operating gathering uncoupled state property measurements of a high quality. This intention host device was placed a few feet from the experimental apparatus, plugged into an electric wall socket (power source) and switched on. For a 110 volt source the electrical power output of the box was less than one microwatt.

Figure 2 illustrates the general time-dependence of the particular property measurement change as a function of space exposure-time to the corresponding imprint intention-host device. Here, we find that nothing much happens in the first 1-2 months (t_1=1-2 months), then the property measurement changes in a sigmoidal fashion, always in the direction intended, and asymptotically levels off, generally at the intended magnitude of change (t_2~3 months). In simple equation form, if $Q_M(t)$ is the magnitude of the property being measured, then we find that

$$Q_M(t) = Q_e + \alpha_{eff}(t)Q_m, \qquad (1)$$

where Q_e is the uncoupled state magnitude of our electric charge atom/molecule world, Q_m is the uncoupled state magnitude of our physical vacuum, information wave world as influenced by the intention-host device, α_{eff} is the magnitude of the coupling coefficient between the two worlds and t is time. When $|\alpha_{eff}| \sim 0$, $Q_M \to Q_e$, our normal reality; when $0.05 \leq |\alpha_{eff}| \leq 1$, Q_M is appreciably changed either

13

up or down according to the sign of the intention. Our present experimental data indicates that the specific intention alters only Q_m and not Q_c.

Four serious experiments have been reported on[1,2] and one has to date been replicated in ten different laboratories in the U.S. and Europe[3]. These are:

(1) To increase the pH of water in equilibrium with air by +1 pH units and with no intentional chemical additions,

(2) To decrease the pH of the same type of water in equilibrium with air by -1 pH units and with no intentional chemical additions,

(3) To significantly increase the in vitro thermodynamic activity of the liver enzyme alkaline phosphatase (ALP) via a 30 minute exposure to an intention-host device "conditioned" space and

(4) To significantly increase the in vivo ATP/ADP ratio in the cells of living fruit fly larvae via lifetime exposure (~28 days) to an intention-host device "conditioned" space so that they would become more physically fit and thus exhibit a significantly reduced larval development time, ▯, to the adult

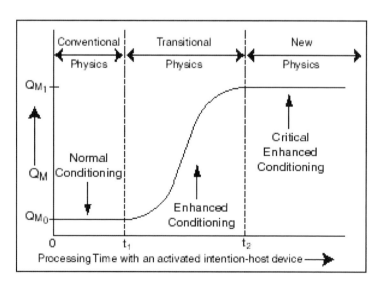

fly stage.

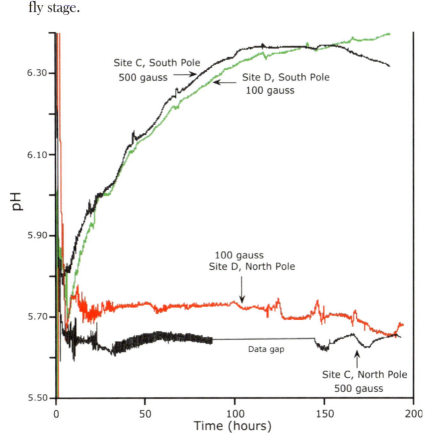

Figure 3.pH changes with time for pure water for both N-pole up and S-pole up axially aligned DC magnetic fields at 100 and 500 gauss)

All four of these experiments were robustly successful with #3 increasing ~25% to 30% at p<0.001 and with #4 (a) ATP/ADP increasing 15% to 20% at p<0.001 and (b) decreasing ~ -25% at p<0.001.

We utilized our pH-measurement system with a disk-shaped ceramic magnet placed symmetrically under the water vessel, first with one magnetic pole pointing upwards into the water vessel for several days and then with the opposite pole pointing upwards for the same time period, in order to detect any differences between the <u>uncoupled state</u>

space conditioning and the coupled state space conditioning. For the former, there was no change in pH for either polarity as one might expect because, in our normal physical reality, although we have electric monopoles of both + and − charge, we have only magnetic dipoles and even numbered magnetic multipoles whose energy and force effects are independent of spatial orientation. However, for a coupled state space conditioning, the picture is quite different as illustrated via Figure 3. (*Figure 3*.pH changes with time for pure water for both N-pole up and S-pole up axially aligned DC magnetic fields at 100 and 500 gauss).

This is the kind of result one would expect if the electromagnetic gauge symmetry state of the space had been lifted from the U(1) level for the uncoupled state space to the SU(2) level for a coupled state space where magnetic monopole charges appear to become accessible via pH-measurement instrumentation. Continued exploration of human subjects via the use of advanced kinesiological techniques and a world class kinesiologist[3], also demonstrated a DC-magnetic field polarity effect wherein the S-pole of a bar magnet held about 1 centimeter from a muscle-group on the body greatly strengthened the testing arm whereas the N-pole of the same magnet located in the same location greatly weakened the testing arm. We have deduced from this result that the human acupuncture meridian system is already functioning at the coupled state level of physical reality. Thus, an individual's specific unconscious or conscious intentions can modulate the flow of subtle energies (Qi) in their own meridians which, in turn, nourish the electromagnetic energy flows in their coarse (U(1) gauge) physical body.

Finally, to bring an end to this introductory background section, we found a theoretical procedure for calculating the excess thermodynamic free energy change, $\delta G_{H^+}{}^*$, of the aqueous H^+-ion when an experimental space transitions from the uncoupled state to the coupled state of physical reality via use of an imprinted intention-host device.

Figure 4 illustrates some gathered data for three of the ten sites involved in the replication experiment[3]. Here, two of the plots are from an active intention-host site (Payson, Arizona) and two are from control sites ~5000 miles to 6000 miles away where no intention-host device was ever present (U.K. and Italy). We found in this study[3] that serious spatial information entanglement occurs between active sites and control sites whether they are 100 meters, 2 to 20 miles, ~1500 miles or 6000 miles apart in space-time without any ability to completely shield the control sites from the active sites. This type of information entanglement appears to be very different from quantum entanglement processes.

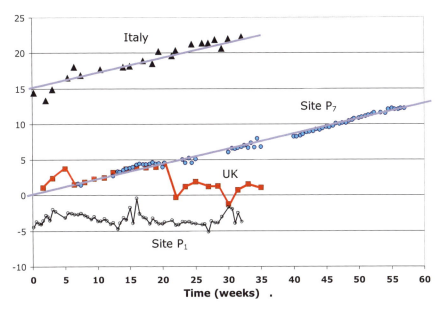

Figure 4. $\delta G^*_{II}+$ vs. time at four diverse sites.

It is this particular type of subtle energy detector[6] that we will be using in our investigation of the Eric Pearl Reconnective Healing workshops in the pages to follow.

Subtle Energy Detection via pH-Measurement

Almost two decades ago, one of us[7] defined subtle energies as all those energies of nature beyond those creating the four fundamental forces of today's orthodox science (gravity, electromagnetism, the weak nuclear force and the strong nuclear force). So how can these subtle energies be detected and quantitatively measured? For this we need to recall Equation 1 and reference 6.

We start with the definition of pH as

$$pH = -\log_{10}(a_{H^+})$$
(2a)

for the U(1) state where a_{H^+} is the thermodynamic activity of the hydrogen ion, H^+, and $\log_{10}$ is the logarithm to the base 10. In experimental practice, Figure 5 provides a schematic set-up of the apparatus used in all of our test-site measurements[6], with the medium of investigation being some type of aqueous solution and a sensor probe involving both a pH-electrode and a water temperature sensor.

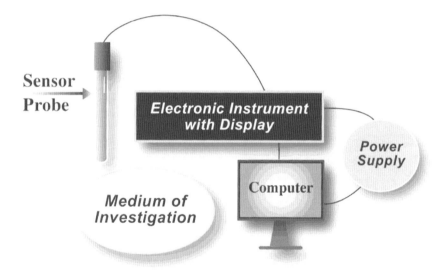

Figure 5. Experimental set-up for testing pH changes.

The physical aspect of pH measurement involves a device that connects (1) a unit H^+ activity standard chemical cell to (2) an aqueous solution vessel whose H^+ activity is to be measured via (3) an H^+-permeable membrane between (1) and (2). As the H^+-ion redistributes itself in this system to produce thermodynamic equilibrium throughout the system, an electric voltage, V_E, develops across the membrane/space charge interface.

The general Boltzmann equilibrium equation connecting V_E to $pH_{U(1)}$ can be readily calculated[6] to give, for an ideal system,

$$V_E = V_0 - 59.16 pH \text{ (mV)} \qquad (2b)$$

where V_0 is the standard cell voltage in the sensor of Figure 5. For the non-ideal case involving membrane interface polarization and other correction factors, Equation 2b becomes

$$VE = S^*(pHU(1)-7)Tcorr \text{ where } Tcorr = (T+273.15)/298.15. \qquad (2c)$$

Here, $V_0 = 7S^*$ and S^* is the electrode slope with respect to pH and voltage determined via calibration. Periodic determination of S^* by calibration is always required to attain accurate measurements.

Rearranging Equation 2c, we define the Nernst parameter, N, to honor that great physical chemist of the 1800's, where

$$N = \frac{S^*}{V_E}(pH - 7)T_{corr}. \qquad (2d)$$

Of course, N should be equal to unity for the U(1) state (the uncoupled state of physical reality). However, as one "conditions" a space via an intention-host device from the U(1) gauge state to the SU(2) gauge state (the partially coupled state of physical reality as in Figure 1.), one finds that $N \neq 1$ and that $|N-1|$ is a direct measure of $|\alpha_{eff}|$ in Equation 1.

For the partially coupled state of physical reality, the electromagnetic gauge symmetry state of the space is changing from the U(1) state towards the SU(2) state which is a higher thermodynamic free energy condition for the space. Thus, Equation 2c must be altered because Figure 6 now holds[6]. When one does this and follows the earlier theoretical procedure, one is able to take the pH-measurement data for the partially coupled state of a space and directly extract $\Box G_H{+}^*(t)$-plots. This is exactly what we have done during our investigations of the four Reconnective-Healing workshops to follow.

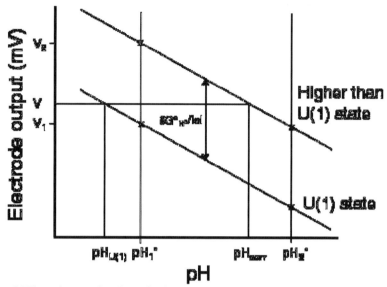

Figure 6.The electrode electrical output vs. pH plots for both the U(1) state ($\partial G^* = 0$) and a higher than U(1) EM gauge symmetry state.

Experimental Protocols and Results

Test 1

Our first experimental test was at the Sedona workshop in February, 2006. Greg Fandel first tested the detector equipment in the Payson lab about 80 miles away and it performed well as had been our experience for several years at that site. He then drove the 1.5 hours to Sedona and set up the detector equipment in the large hotel room where the healing workshop was to take place about 5-6 hours later. Greg had difficulty in recalibrating the pH-measurement part of the system because the value of S in Equation 2c was falling outside the range of the normal pH calibration specifications. Eventually the system settled down to a degree so that pH and temperature measurements could commence. The next 9 hours of data-gathering is shown in Figure 7.

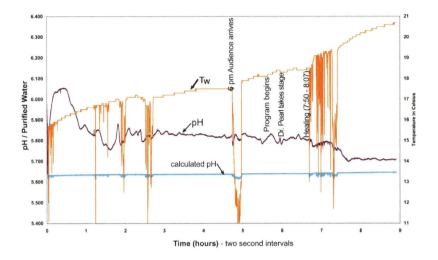

Figure 7. Very anomalous water temperature, T_W, behavior was observed at this Sedona, healing workshop.

Here, the uppermost curve, T_W, is the water temperature; the middle curve is the measured pH while the bottom curve is the theoretically calculated pH, $pH_{U(t)}$, which, following Equation 1 for both T_W and pH, are

$$T_M(t) = T_e(t) + \square_{eff} T_m, \qquad (3a)$$

$$pH_M(t) = pH_{U(t)}(t) + \square pH_m(t), \qquad (3b)$$

where

$$pH_{U(t)}(t) = 5.54 + 3.12 \times 10^{-3} T_e(t), \qquad (3c)$$

and T_e is in °C. at an air CO_2 partial pressure of 380 ppm.

The T_W anomalies (downward shooting lines) in Figure 7 started to appear ~5 hours before the audience arrived in the large room and ended ~4 hours after they entered. These temperature measurement instabilities are revealed by the downward plunging lines in the T_W-plot. We have experienced this kind of phenomenon in our Payson

Science Confirms Reconnective Healing

lab many times before and have found this type of anomaly to correlate strongly with the presence of high $\delta G_{H}+^{*}$-values.

It is important for the reader to realize that this T_W –data indicates that this space had somehow been lifted to a very high EM gauge symmetry state well before any of the workshop participants entered that room (information entanglement in time??). When a pH-calibration cycle was carried out with the detector in this same room ~1 week after the workshop event, absolutely no anomalies at all appeared in either the T_W or pH plots and the room appeared to be completely back to its normal reality, the U(1) gauge symmetry state.

Analysis of this raw data to create a $\delta G_{H}+^{*}(t)$ plot occurred about 1.5 weeks later for this workshop room space. At time t=0, $\delta G_{H}+^{*}$ was found to be almost double what it would have been if δ_{eff} in Equation 1 had been zero. At its peak (almost two days later) it had almost tripled the δ_{eff} ~0 value and, ~1.5 weeks later, it had decayed back to ~double again. If one asks the question "How much would one have had to "heat" this room from an δ_{eff}=0 state to yield its maximum $\delta G_{H}+^{*}$-state as found via our detector and describe the result as an effective temperature change, δT_{eff}, as given in Figure 8, one notes that it would have required a change in effective temperature over the workshop period by ~300 °C. However, the actual change in workshop room temperature was no more than ~5-10 °C. One implication of this result is that the $\delta GH+^{*}$ occurring here is that due to an increased information creation process, which means a thermodynamic entropy decreasing rather that a thermodynamic energy increasing process, was taking place.

When I talked about a week or so later with one of the healers who had attended this workshop, she indicated that, during this workshop, her subjectively-assessed healing abilities felt as if they were ~3 to 5 times stronger than normal.

Science Confirms Reconnective Healing

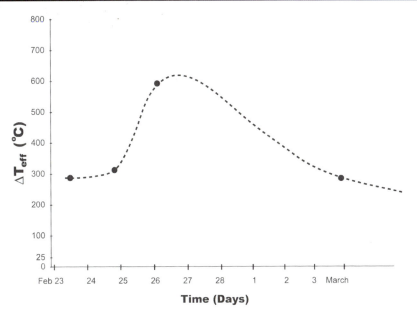

Figure 8. Possible data plot of the excess thermodynamic free energy for the healing workshop room as a function of time via converting δG_{II}^+ to an energy equivalent, effective change in temperature, ΔT_{eff}, for a normal room.

Test 2

Two complete sets of our standard T_W and pH measurement equipment plus a high resolution (0.001 °C.) temperature probe for measuring air temperature, T_A, was driven from our Payson lab to the Sheraton Universal Hotel in Los Angeles (~500 miles) on July 25, 2007. The pH-electrodes were continuously kept in freshly purified water throughout the entire 8-day Payson/Los Angeles/Payson trip by Walter Dibble, Jr., except for when they were calibrated in L.A.

One of the main experimental goals was to quantitatively determine the existing degree of space conditioning above the purely U(1) gauge state prior to, during and after the main workshop events. One of the detector systems was set up on July 26 and continuously operated during the day in the Studio I room (for 2 days). Data, sampled at 10 second intervals was recorded via a laptop computer. This data revealed a pre-existing room space conditioning of ~-5± 1/2 meV

(δT_{eff} ~60°C.) was present at least two days prior to any workshop activity.

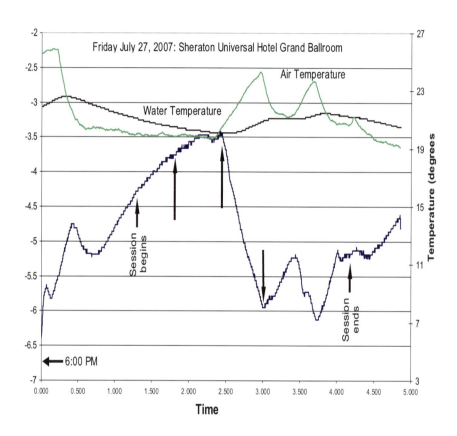

Figure 9. $\delta G^*_{II}{}^+$ for the space vs. time.

Science Confirms Reconnective Healing

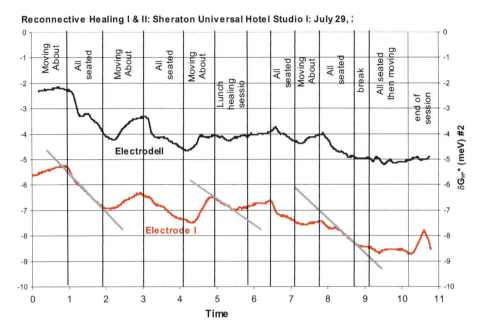

Figure 10. $\delta G^*_{II^+}$ for the space vs. time.

On the evening of July 27, this detector was moved to the Grand Ballroom (about 30 meters away from Studio I) in order to monitor Dr. Eric Pearl's evening lecture to the group of student healers convening for the following two-day workshop. Figure 9 provides simultaneous $T_W(t)$, $T_A(t)$ and $\delta G_{II^+}^*(t)$ plots for a 5-hour period surrounding this event. Although, at 6:00 PM, the ballroom started out at $\delta G_{II^+}^* \sim -6.5$ meV, it had increased to ~ -4.5 meV by the time the session actually began and, although T_A (and especially T_W) changed by no more than ~ 0.5 °C., δT_{eff} had changed by $\sim +20$ °C. The relatively linear drop in δT_{eff} by ~ -30 °C. and increase in T_A by $\sim +4$ °C., between 8:30 PM and 9:00 PM, when Dr. Pearl was performing subtle energy work onstage, appears to indicate that a $\delta(TS)$ thermodynamic free energy term of the informational/entropic, S, type is strongly correlated with the process. One should also note, especially after 8:30 PM, how the $\delta G_{II^+}^*$-value is <u>more responsive</u> to

25

T_A than to T_W. This may indicate a shift from pH-electrode "conditioning" to anti-phase space "conditioning".

On July 28 and 29, both detector systems were set up in the Studio I room to monitor the levels 1 and 2 workshops. Figure 10, showing data for the 29th, indicates that each electrode has its own "personality" (depends on electrode history, make and manufacturer) with electrode I being more responsive than electrode II. Following the electrode data, one notices a strong correlation between the periods of an almost constant downward slope of $\delta GH+^*$ with time when either Dr. Pearl or the teaching assistants were lecturing on stage. It appears as if an entrained coherence between the on-stage speaker and the audience is meaningfully controlling the pH-measurement equipment. This entrained coherence is broken via the speaker and audience moving about the room causing a reversal of any downward pH trend.

Test 3

The Tucson, 2008 Level I and II workshop event occurred over the weekend of August 15-17 while the level III event occurred on the 18th and 19th, all at the Conference Center of the Sheraton Four Points Hotel. Three sets of our $\delta G_{H}+^*$-detector and two high-resolution temperature probes were driven from Payson to Tucson with the pH-electrodes continuously in freshly purified water. One of the detector systems was eventually used with the pH-water bottle being open to the air while the other two were eventually used with the water bottle being closed to air. All the water had time to equilibrate with air before and during the trip to Tucson. The closed water bottles were to test for possible pH-variation that might result from variations in the CO_2 level present in the seminar rooms as people came and went during the day.

Figure 11, includes the Thursday pre-event measurements followed by a ~12 hour overnight disassembling and reassembling of the detector system at ~8 AM on Friday and at the big Friday evening event of Dr. Pearl's lecture. Once again we first see a small amount of supposedly pre-conditioning of the space on Thursday which is decaying towards

Science Confirms Reconnective Healing

zero. On Friday, the reassembled equipment starts out with a pH of ~-4 meV which slowly diminishes in magnitude over time until the "Friday evening lecture" effect via Eric Pearl sets in. Once again the ~12 hour overnight detector system disassembling and Saturday morning reassembling occurs with the detector system seemingly picking up were it left off the previous evening and continuing its decrease in δGH^{+*} towards -9 meV.

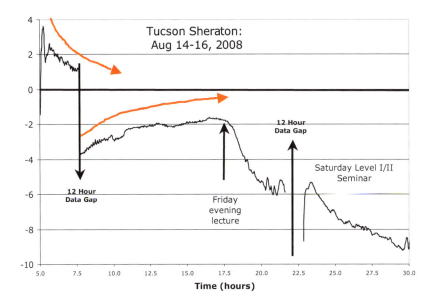

Figure 11. $\delta G^*_{II^+}$ for the space vs. time.

The curved arrows represent our best guess of where the data was headed before some significant change occurred.

The interesting Sunday, August 17 data shown in Figure 12 is very consistent with the Figure 10-data of July 29, 2007; however, two important factors need to be noticed here: (1) the very steep linear gradients in slope of δGH^{+*} with time during stage presentations in the afternoon are much larger in magnitude than for both the morning session and for the Figure 10 case and (2) a marked correlation exists between the two large blips in T_A and the two stage-presentation downward drops in δG_{II}^{+*}. The similarities between the open-to-air

27

pH water bottles and the air-tight pH water bottles strongly suggests that differences in spacetime air CO_2 levels are not being measured.

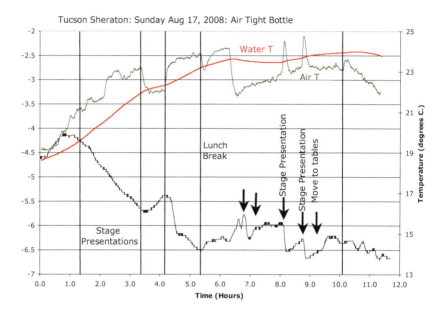

Figure 12. $\delta G^*_{H^+}$ for the space as well as water and air temperature vs. time.

Test 4

The venue was the Universal Hilton in Los Angeles, September, 2008. Once again, WED, Jr. drove a plethora of measurement equipment from our Payson Laboratory to Los Angeles. Four $\delta G^*_{H^+}$-detector systems and three high-resolution temperature probes were set up in the Plaza Suite room on Thursday September 11, 2008, one day before the Friday evening opening event. Figure 13 represents about 3 days worth of continuous data spaced out over a week. This data is similar to previous measurements of the "Friday Lecture Effect" with some notable new features. Most of the data gaps, once again, are due to the equipment being shut down and stowed overnight, then reactivated the next day. What is new here is the first 24-hour measurement in the Plaza Suite. This is the first time we were able to acquire a <u>continuous</u> 24-hour set of data (overnight) at one of these venues. After the electrode was calibrated at hour zero, there was roughly a 6-hour "settling in" period before the value leveled out. The value of ~-1.5 meV may actually represent the "real" background conditioning value for this room. The room was unoccupied for most of this 24-hour period. An interesting event occurred early in the morning on Friday (well before anyone entered the room) when there was a sudden break downward in $\delta G^*_{II}+$-values with an almost linear slope. Could this be the onset of the "Friday Night Lecture Effect" starting at this time? The equipment was then moved to the actual site of the Friday night lecture where the downward slope in $\delta G^*_{II}+$-values continued (even steeper) during the lecture event itself.

For the following two days (Saturday and Sunday) the trend in $\delta G^*_{II}+$-values was also strongly down during the measurement periods. The first strong uptrend to be observed in the measurements up to that time began near the end of the session on Sunday. The next day (Monday) the $\delta G^*_{II}+$-values started out much higher (following the trend of the previous days ending period?). Once again the curved arrows represent our best guess of where the data was headed before the equipment was shut down overnight. This data strongly suggests a return to zero space conditioning on Monday and Tuesday.

Before closing this section, it is important to recognize that, as we have moved from Test 1 through Tests 2 and 3 to Test 4, we have steadily increased the multiplicity of individual measurement systems applied to the data-gathering process. Thus, the issue of <u>information entanglement</u> between these various individual sub-systems becomes important and one is in danger of "washing out" the magnitude of uniquely different effects via the out-of-phase coupling between different components of the overall measurement system. This is not a problem for the various Q_e-parts in the Equation 1 mathematical formalism because they are basically scalar quantities (only one number is needed to define a property at a specific point in space). However, the individual factors that ultimately make up Q_m in Equation 1 are all vectors or tensors (one needs three or more numbers to define a property at a specific point in space) and these need to be added together in a special way (head to tail arrangement for vectors) even for one detector system. When there are four measurement systems operating simultaneously in the same space, the vector components of one detector information entangle with those of the other detectors because of the necessary vector addition and multiplication processes involved in the evaluation of Q_m and thus $\delta G^*_{II^+}$. The mathematics is doable but tedious and not appropriate for this paper.

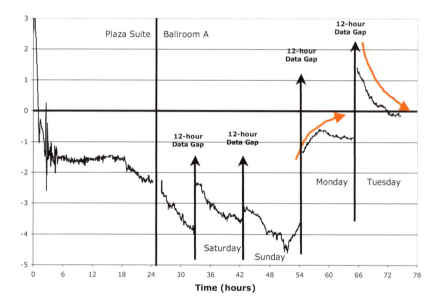

Figure 13. $\delta G^*_{II^+}$ for the space vs. time. The curved arrows represent our best guess of where the data was headed before the equipment was disassembled and reassembled.

It is also appropriate to point out that, even within <u>one</u> detector system measuring the partially coupled state of physical reality, at least two kinds of "conditioning" need to be discriminated: (1) The pH-electrode change[6] and (2) a change in the room space itself relative to the uncoupled state reality. Thus, the <u>actual</u> measured value of $\delta G^*_{II^+}$ for a single detector, $\delta G^*_{II^+}(M)$, is given by

$$\delta G^*_{II^+}(M) = \delta G^*_{II^+}(E) + \delta G^*_{II^+}(s) \qquad (4)$$

where E refers to "electrode" and s refers to "space". It should be noted that, in Figure 4, $\delta G^*_{H^+}$ refers to $\delta G^*_{H^+}(M)$ whereas in Figure 9 through 13, $\delta G^*_{H^+}$ refers to $\delta G^*_{H^+}(s)$.

Some Closing Observations and Comments

1. During speaker on-stage presentations to the audience, one observes that the magnitude of $\delta G^*_{H^+}$ always seems to increase at ~ a constant slope with time. This signals positive information production and thus thermodynamic entropy annihilation,

2. During audience standing, moving around and talking, the magnitude of $\delta^*_{H^+}$ always seems to decrease. This signals that net excess positive entropy production is occurring,

3. The periods of audience-focused attention upon the on-stage speaker signals that group entrainment leading to significant growth of group coherence is occurring. This leads to high information production rate events,

4. Substantial evidence was found for pre-event room "conditioning". Such events may be concrete examples of macroscopic temporal information entanglement,

5. Macroscopic spatial information entanglement due to simultaneous use of multiple measuring instruments appear to be generating reduced contrast in the magnitudes of various event signatures. This probably occurs via the addition of out-of-phase vector components (a type of data randomization) and

6. Clear highly correlated entrainment of $T_A(M)$ and $\delta G^*_{H^+}(s)$ plots have been observed.

References

1. W. A. Tiller, W. E. Dibble, Jr., and M. J. Kohane, Conscious Acts of Creation: The Emergence of a New Physics (Pavior Publishing, Walnut Creek, CA, USA, 2001).

2. Tiller W. A., Dibble W. E. Jr., "New experimental data revealing an unexpected dimension to materials science and engineering", *Materials Research Innovations*, 5, 21-34 (2001).

3. W. A. Tiller, W. E. Dibble, Jr. and J. G. Fandel, Some Science Adventures with Real Magic (Pavior Publishing, Walnut Creek, CA, USA, 2005).

4. W. A. Tiller, Psychoenergetic Science: A Second Copernican-Scale Revolution (Pavior Publishing, Walnut Creek, CA, USA, 2007).

5. W. A. Tiller, W. E. Dibble, Jr. and C. T. Krebs, "Instrumental response to advanced kinesiological treatments in a 'conditioned' space", *Subtle Energies and Energy Medicine*, 13 (2), 21-108 (2004).

6. W. A.Tiller and W. E. Dibble, Jr. "Toward general experimentation and discovery in "conditioned" laboratory and complementary and alternative medicine spaces: Part V. Data on 10 different sites using a robust new type of subtle energy detector". *J Altern Complement Med*, 13, 133-149 (2007).

7. W. A. Tiller, "What are subtle energies?", *J. Sci. Expl.*, 7, 293 (1993).

Science Confirms Reconnective Healing

Dr. Ann Linda Baldwin and Dr. Gary E. Schwartz

3. Baseline Testing of Reconnective Healing Practitioners During Self-Healing

University of Arizona, Tucson,

[1] Laboratory for the Advances in Consciousness and Health, Department of Psychology, abaldwin@u.arizona.edu [2] Department of Physiology, College of Medicine

Introduction

Energy Healers use specific states of consciousness to heal others and themselves through manipulation of the Human Energy Field. Although the Human Energy Field has not yet been adequately described by the scientific method, it is experienced by Energy Healers as a field of energy that informs and interpenetrates the human body and that can be influenced by un-ordinary states of consciousness called "healing intention". One obstacle inherent in the scientific study of Energy Healing is the wide variety of traditions in which Energy Healers are trained, resulting in healers of different capabilities, using varied techniques. The long-term purpose of this study is to gather information on the characteristics of Energy Healers, across healers of various traditions, so that future studies of Energy Healing may be scientifically standardized, ultimately leading to a better scientific understanding of this form of medicine. In addition, it is hoped that physiological and psychological markers, if they exist, will enable scientist to more accurately assess energy healers for competence when they select subjects to participate in the scientific process.

Practitioners of energy healing modalities such as Reiki are encouraged to practice on themselves as well as on others, and they are adept at sensing the energy flow though their own bodies. Previous research has focused on self-healing because the experiments are simple to implement and involve fewer variables. In a preliminary study involving Reiki practitioners (Baldwin, 2007), the healers showed increased cutaneous blood flow in the fingertips during self-healing. The finger blood vessels are richly innervated with adrenoreceptors which cause sympathetically-mediated vasoconstriction (Muck-Weymann et al, 1996). Therefore, the observed increase in cutaneous blood flow when Reiki practitioners self-heal, demonstrates a reduction in sympathetic stimulation of these vessels, indicative of relaxation. Another study, on computer operators trained in Qigong, showed that practice of Qigong (a self-healing modality) reduced heart rate and noradrenaline excretion in the urine, also indicative of a relaxation response (Skoglund and Jansson, 2007).

There is another energy healing modality, Reconnnective Healing, that is rapidly gaining in popularity, worldwide. For this reason it was decided to extend the previous studies on Reiki self-healing to include this modality. Reconnective Healing is said to connect people to a new set of vibrational frequencies that stimulate healing of the body, mind and spirit by promoting a return to balance. In practical terms, Reconnective Healers work with their hands to sense and manipulate the electromagnetic biofields of the people being healed. Although the concept of biofields is still controversial, fetal heart biofields have been measured routinely using extremely sensitive magnetic detectors (Seki, 2008) and there is a biophysical basis for the existence of biofields (Movaffaghi and Farsi, 2008; Rein, 2004). Reconnective Healers concentrate equally on healing others, as well as themselves. During training they practice on others so they are used to sensing their own energy fields as well as energy fields of other people. The information gained from this study will allow us to better describe the specific characteristics of Reconnective Healers and by using a moderately large sample size, to accurately statistically document the results.

Presently there are several ongoing studies to investigate the effects of Reconnective Healing on the healers and on their surroundings, but so far no papers have appeared in peer-reviewed journals. The purpose of this study was to characterize the effects of Reconnective

Healing on the autonomic system (ANS) of the practitioners as they sensed and manipulated their body biofield. Based on previous results with Reiki and Qigong it was hypothesized that Reconnective Healing would promote a relaxation response in the practitioners.

Methods

Experimental Design: Each subject was seated and the following instructions were read to them: "We are going to be taking some perfusion Images and measure your heart rate variability. These are non-invasive measures and there is nothing that you have to do. Please relax while we take the measures. We will be taking measurements from a distance. We will take four images of your right hand. One baseline image, two when you are allowing the flow of energy and one after you have stopped the flow of energy. You may use your left hand to sense the energy field of the hand being scanned when the energy is flowing if you wish. Please place you hand on the mat and we will begin". A plethysmograph (pulse sensor) was clipped to the subject's ear lobe for measurement of HRV. The sensor was attached to a computer via an emWavePC (HeartMath LLC) device. The right hand of each subject was scanned by a Laser Doppler Perfusion Imaging System (PeriScan PIM II imager, Perimed, Sweden) to measure any changes in cutaneous blood perfusion occurring within the healer's palm. The palm was placed about 10 inches below the scanner and 4 images were obtained, each image taking 2.5 minutes. Thus, the baseline period lasted 2.5 minutes, the self-healing period (ON1, ON2) 5 minutes, and the post period, when subjects were asked to stop the energy flow (OFF), 2.5 minutes.

Experimental Subjects: Measurements were performed on 50 advanced Reconnective Healers (Level III or above) who were attending Reconnective Healing Seminars in Tucson (August 15-17, 2008) and in Los Angeles (July/August, 2007 and September 18-21, 2008). This group included 14 males and 36 females in the age-range 38 to 68 (males) and 31 to 69 (females). The investigation was carried out with the approval of the University of Arizona Human Subjects Protection Committee and informed consent was obtained from each subject after the study procedures had been explained.

Experimental Measures

Heart Rate Variability: The HRV is due to the complementary relationship between the sympathetic and parasympathetic branches of the autonomic nervous system (Malik, 1996). Thus measuring HRV is a non-invasive method for quantifying the state of the ANS. In normal, healthy subjects under control conditions there is some variability in heart rate and blood pressure. Instruments used for recording HRV analyze the signal by means of time domain or frequency domain (spectral analysis), both of which quantify the amount of variability in heart rate that exists in a given recording. In the time domain, parameters of HRV include SDRR, the standard deviation of the inter-beat interval (IBI), which gives a gross measure of HRV, and the root mean square of the SDRR (RMSSD), which reflects the parasympathetic stimulation of the ANS. High HRV is associated with social engagement in humans (Porges, 2003).

In order to accurately identify the sympathetic versus parasympathetic components of HRV, frequency domain measures are required. To transform IBI data to the frequency domain, a fast Fourier transform (FFT) is performed on the data so that the HRV is expressed in terms of the frequencies of the variation. In humans the frequencies fall into three distinct ranges, very low frequency (VLF: 0 - 0.04 Hz), low frequency (LF: 0.04 - 0.15 Hz), and high frequency (HF: 0.15 - 0.4 Hz) (McCraty et al, 1995). The variation within a certain frequency range is expressed in terms of its power, which is related to the square of the amplitude of the signal. The VLF power reflects sympathetic stimulation, the LF power reflects both sympathetic and parasympathetic activities, and the HF power reflects parasympathetic activity. The LF/HF ratio is used to quantify the overall balance between the sympathetic and parasympathetic systems.

In this study, the emWavePC program was used to output inter-beat interval (HR) data to a text file which was then analyzed in more detail using a free HRV program (KubiosHRV) available on the internet: http://kubios.uku.fi/

Blood Perfusion of Palm: Three fleshy areas of the palm were analyzed: (1) the rectangular region beneath the base of fingers; (2)

the mound at base of thumb; (3) the fleshy area extending below the little finger. An initial visual examination of the palm images obtained, prior to analysis, showed that these regions demonstrated the most change in perfusion throughout the experiment, whereas the central area of the palm usually showed very low blood perfusion with almost no variation whether or not healing was being performed. Three 'Regions of Interest' (ROI) were drawn on each image, using a cursor, to outline the three areas of palm to be analyzed. A sample image is shown in Figure 1.

Image Analysis: All data were automatically exported to an Excel spreadsheet and the mean perfusion was calculated for each ROI by the software provided with the perfusion imager. Mean perfusion, expressed as a percentage of the initial reference image, was plotted as a function of time in each case.

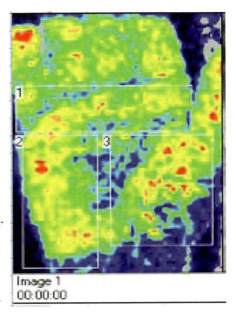

Figure 1: Sample image of palm scanned by perfusion imager, showing the three regions of interest (ROI). Red, yellow, green, blue represent high to low blood flow.

Statistics: Statistical tests (Repeated Measures Analysis of Variance followed by pair-wise multiple comparisons by the Tukey test) were run to determine significant differences between each parameter (% increase in perfusion, HR, HRV) when compared between each part of the experimental session (whether sensing the field or not). Since this was a 'within subjects" design, each subject acted as their own control. A probability value < 0.05 was considered to be statistically significant.

Results

Heart Rate Variability: There was a highly significant decrease in HRV (p<0.001) during sensing as compared to baseline, as measured by the standard deviation of inter-beat interval (SDRR) and by the percentage of inter-beat intervals in which the previous inter-beat interval differed in length from the subsequent one by more than 50 ms (pnn50). Average values of SDRR (ms) fell from 0.051 ± 0.004 (SE) to 0.039 ± 0.002 and pnn50 fell from 12.19% ± 1.85 to 8.15% ± 1.24. During the post-sensing period, there was a significant increase in HRV back to, or towards, its baseline value (SDRR, 0.052 ± 0.007, p<0.02; pnn50, 9.96% ± 1.48, p<0.04). The change in HRV is illustrated in Figure 2 (upper panel), showing a sample plot of inter-beat-interval as a function of time. The shaded region in the middle corresponds to the time period during which the subject was sensing their field. This result was highly reproducible among the practitioners tested. *There was also a significant increase in heart rate (bpm) (p<0.001) during sensing (77.65 ± 1.92 (SE) compared to baseline 74.3 ± 1.55, which returned close to its baseline value after sensing stopped (75.57 ± 1.47, p<0.001).* In addition, the act of sensing produced a significant decrease in the root mean square of the standard deviation of the inter-beat intervals (RMSSD) (ms), from 41.47 ± 5.01 (SE) to 31.36 ± 2.09, (p<0.001) that did not return to normal after sensing stopped (32.94 ± 2.43). *This finding reflects a strong decrease in parasympathetic nervous activity during sensing.* The low frequency power of HRV (ms^2) (LF) was significantly lower during sensing (561.3 ± 67.3) compared to baseline (1064.8 ± 207.5 (SE), p<0.005) and then returned close to baseline values when sensing stopped (1058.8 ± 193.7, p<0.02). The LF power reflects both the sympathetic and parasympathetic nervous activity. The high frequency (HF) power of HRV (ms^2) was significantly lower during sensing (404.2 ± 64.9) compared to baseline (674.7 ± 159.1, p<0.01) and then returned close to baseline values when sensing stopped (603.7 ± 115.4, p<0.04). High frequency power reflects parasympathetic nervous activity, and this result is consistent with the decrease in RMSSD during sensing.

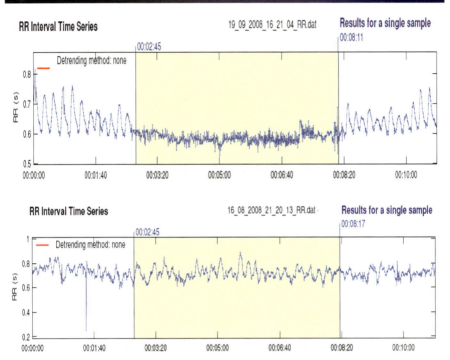

Figure 2: *Sample plot of inter-beat interval (s) as a function of time (minutes/seconds) from experienced Reconnective Healer (Upper Panel). Shaded portion represents time period of 'sensing'. Note decrease in mean HRV and in mean IBI during sensing period. A decrease in IBI represents an increase in heart rate. Sample plot of inter-beat interval (s) as a function of time (minutes/seconds) from subject with no energy healing experience (Lower Panel). Note no noticeable change in mean HRV or mean IBI throughout recording period.*

At one of the seminars (Tucson), we were able to take measurements of HRV on 9 people who had no experience of Reconnective Healing or any other type of energy healing. They had arrived early to attend the Level I/II seminar and therefore had not experienced the seminar prior to measurement. The HRV measurements lasted for 10 minutes, similar to the protocol for the experienced healers, but these subjects were just asked to sit still for the whole period. The naive subjects were of a similar age range (30-61) and gender distribution (2 males and 7 females) as the experienced healers. When the HRV recordings were each separated into 3 different time periods, correlated to the pre-sensing, sensing and post-sensing periods used in the protocol for the experienced healers, and then analyzed, no significant differences were found for any of the parameters compared between time periods. The lack of change in HRV is illustrated in Figure 2 (lower panel), showing a sample plot of inter-beat-interval as a function of time. However, for **SDRR** and **HF** power, the statistical power of the test was less than the desired value of 0.8 due to the small number of participants, and so these results must be treated with caution. It could be argued that the small hand movements sometimes involved in sensing of the field could have produced the reduction in HRV seen in experienced healers. However, in initial pilot studies it was demonstrated that such movements did not affect HRV.

Blood Perfusion of Palm: When all data were considered as percentage change in perfusion compared to baseline versus time (images obtained during first half of sensing (ON1), second half of sensing (ON2) and when sensing stopped (OFF)), there was no significant variation with time, that is, the sensing did not significantly alter the blood perfusion in the palm of the hand being scanned. However, it was noticed that 19 people showed a decrease in perfusion (less blood perfusion in palm) during ON1 compared to the baseline reference image, and 31 people showed an increase in perfusion. We were interested to see whether the 19 people who showed a decrease during ON1 actually started off with a high blood perfusion in the palm at baseline, and vice versa for the 31 people who showed an increase during ON1. We predicted that the people who started off high would not show further increases and might show decreases when sensing started, whereas the people who started low might show an increase in perfusion during the sensing. Of the 19 people who showed a decrease in blood perfusion during the healing, 14 of them started off with high blood perfusion in the baseline image, consistent with our prediction. The criteria for the presence of high blood perfusion in the reference image were:

1. Two out of the three ROI's (palm areas) must contain more of a trace of red in the image.

2. The overall background color of the image of the palm must be green and not blue.

Statistical analysis showed that the people who started off with low blood perfusion showed an average increase in intensity of about 8% on sensing (ON1) whereas people who started off with a high blood perfusion showed an average decrease in intensity of about 5%. *This effect was highly significant (p<0.00003) and is consistent with the idea of Reconnective Healing bringing systems back into balance.* However, this initial response could also be just a physiological adjustment to the temperature of the room. One question is 'why did some people start off with high blood perfusion, i.e. hot hands?' The people with hot hands mostly came for measurement at sequential times on a given day, and so it is possible that they had all had a similar response to something that happened during a certain class in the workshop.

When all the subjects were considered together, there was a significant difference in the way that the perfusion of the different regions of the palm (ROI's) (averaged over all participants), varied with time (p<0.03) (Figure 3). All three ROI's showed an increase in intensity from sensing ON1 to ON2 but this increase was not statistically significant. For ROI1 (across the base of the fingers) the intensity continued to increase after sensing was stopped (OFF) and the increase from ON1 to OFF was marginally statistically significant (p<0.06). For ROI2 and ROI3 the intensities dropped when sensing was stopped, although this change was not statistically significant.

When the same analysis was repeated with people divided into 'start high' and 'start low' blood perfusion sub-groups, similar patterns were seen between the two sub-groups in the variation of perfusion with time for the ROI's. For 'start low' people, (27/50) the perfusion for all ROI's increased by about 7% when sensing started (ON1), and for ROI1, continued to increase significantly with time (ON2, OFF). For ROI2 and ROI3, the perfusions remained fairly constant after the initial increase from baseline to ON1. For 'high start' people (23/50) the perfusion for all the ROI's decreased by about 5% when sensing started (ON1) and the perfusion continued to increase for ROI1 but not for ROI2 and ROI3, similar to the 'low start' people. Thus, after the adjustment of blood perfusion to homeostasis, which may or may not have been caused by the Reconnective Healing process, the changes in perfusion followed the same pattern regardless of the initial conditions, perfusion increasing on average in the region at the base of the fingers (ROI1) during and after sensing. Since this latter response was not related to homeostasis, it appears to be a characteristic of Reconnective Healing. Closer examination of the data showed that this trend was most marked in 25/50 healers who also demonstrated an increase in perfusion of ROI2 and ROI 3 during sensing, followed by a fall after sensing was stopped.

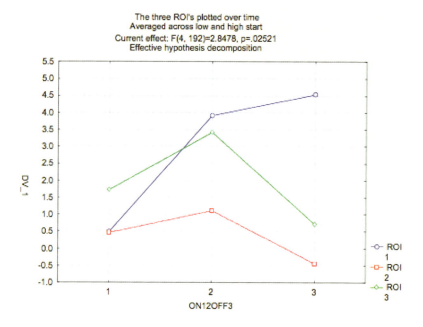

Figure 3: Plot showing variation in intensity (blood perfusion) with time for all 3 ROI's. Data are averaged over all participants. There is a significant difference (p<0.03) between the patterns of time variation for the three ROI's.

Discussion

The results of this study show that self-healing by Reconnective Healers is associated with increased heart rate and decreased heart rate variability, neither of which are indicative of relaxation, and with changes in palm blood flow that promote homeostasis. In light of the previous self-healing studies with Reiki and Qigong, these results are surprising; it is clear from the data that during self-healing, the practitioners demonstrated significantly reduced parasympathetic (PS) activity, which is consistent with exerting mental effort.

There has been one other previously published study investigating the effects of energy healing on HRV (Burleson and Schwartz, 2005). It involved a self-healing protocol with only a small number of people (n=13) who were trained by Rosalyn Bruyere. Bruyere teaches her trainees to 'run energy' (RE) which purportedly draws energy through the body. It was hypothesized that RE would be associated with decreases in PS activity and increases in sympathetic nervous activity. In these experiments, low frequency HRV power increased and high frequency decreased, consistent with the hypothesis. Heart rate did not change. The performance of Reconnective Healing seems to produce a different physiological effect on the healer than does RE, specifically causing a decrease in PS rather than an increase in sympathetic activity, and also significantly increasing heart rate. Unlike Bruyere healers, Reconnective Healers also showed a significant decrease in the low frequency HRV power. Low frequency HRV power reflects stimulation of both the sympathetic and PS branches of the ANS, and so the interpretation of changes in this frequency range is ambiguous. However, the Reconnective Healers also showed, on average, an increase in blood perfusion of the palm during self-healing. Since palm blood flow is reduced by sympathetic stimulation (Yamazaki et al, 2006), these responses suggest that both sympathetic and parasympathetic stimulation were reduced during the self-healing process of Reconnective Healing.

Similar to the action of Reconnective Healing, performance of mental arithmetic produces an increase in heart rate and a decrease in PS; however, unlike Reconnective Healing it also increases sympathetic activity (Yu et al, 2009). One state of mind that is linked to decreased HRV, decreased sympathetic and decreased parasympathetic stimulation is a condition termed "Emotional Quiescence" (McCraty,et al, 2006). As quoted in the cited text, "Emotional Quiescence emerges when certain individuals undergo an extraordinary transition to enter a distinctive heart-focused psychophysiological state. ....The subjective experience of this mode is a state in which the intrusion of mental and emotional chatter is reduced to a point of internal quietness, to be replaced by a profound feeling of peace and serenity simultaneously..... First-person descriptions include a heightened awareness of the movement of energy both within one's body and between oneself and other people." However, in this state, heart rate decreases, contrary to the slight increase observed with Reconnective Healing. Therefore another factor appears to be involved with Reconnective Healing that affects heart rate, possibly related to the slight movement of the hand,

In summary, this study demonstrates that Reconnective Healing applied to the self causes a measurable change in the ANS. The fact that this response was highly reproducible among subjects is evidence of the consistency of the training that they had received in the Reconnective Healing seminars. Unlike some other energy healing modalities, such as Reiki and Qigong, self application of Reconnective Healing does not invoke a relaxation response in the practitioner, but decreases both sympathetic and PS stimulation of the ANS, as observed when a person is in a state of emotional detachment, inner quiet and heightened awareness of the flow of subtle energy. These physiological responses are compatible with the Reconnective Healing principle of sensing and manipulating energy fields, rather than passively allowing the energy to flow through the body, as in Reiki. Thus the monitoring of HRV has proven to be a useful method of demonstrating the way in which subtle energy is accessed when performing different types of energy healing. Further studies will address physiological changes that occur when healers are healing other people, rather than themselves.

References

Baldwin, A.L. (2007). Effects of Reiki and Concentration on Cutaneous Microvascular Perfusion of the Fingers. Focus on Alternative and Complementary Therapies, 12: p6.

Burleson, K.O. and Schwartz, G.E. (2005). Energy healing training and heart rate variability. The Journal of Alternative and Complementary Medicine, 11(3): 391-395.

Malik, M. (1996). Heart rate variability. Standards of measurement, physiological interpretation and clinical use. Circulation, 93: 1043-1065.

McCraty, R., Atkinson, M., Tiller, W.A. Rein, G. & Watkins, A.D. (1995). The effects of emotions on short-term power spectrum analysis of heart rate variability, American Journal of Cardiology, 76(14), 1089-1093.

McCraty, R., Atkinson, M., Tomasino, D. and Bradley, R.T. (2006). The Coherent Heart, HeartMath Research Center, Institute of HeartMath.

Movaffaghi, Z, and Farsi, M. (2008). Biofield Therapies: Biological basis and biological regulations? Complementary Therapies in Clinical Practice, 15: 35-37.

Muck-Weymann, M.E., Albrecht, H.P., Hager, D., Hiller, D., Hornstein, O.P. and Bauer, R.D. (1996). Respiratory-dependent Laser-Doppler flux motion in different skin areas and its meaning to autonomic nervous control of the vessels of the skin. Microvascular Research, 52: 69-78.

Porges, S.W. (2003). Social engagement and attachment: a phylogenetic perspective, Annals of the New York Academy of Sciences:1008, 31-47.

Rein, G. (2004). Bioinformation within the biofield: beyond bioelectromagnetics, The Journal of Alternative and Complementary Medicine, 10(1): 59-68.

Seki, Y., Kandori, A., Kumagai, Y., Ohnuma, M., Ishiyama A., Ishii T., Nakamura Y., Horigome H. and Chiba T. (2008). Unshielded fetal magnetocardiography system using two-dimensional gradiometers, Review of Scientific Instruments,79(3): 036106.

Skoglund, L. and Jansson, E. (2007). Qigong reduces stress in computer operators. Complementary Therapies in Clinical Practice, 13(2): 78-84.

Yamazaki, F. and Sone, R. (2006). Different vascular responses in glabrous and nonglabrous skin with increasing core temperature during exercise. European Journal of Applied Physiology, 97(5): 582-90.

Yu, X., Zhang, J., Xie D., Wang, J. and Zhang, C. (2009). Relationship between scalp potential and autonomic nervous activity during a mental arithmetic task. Autonomic Neuroscience. Basic and Clinical, (in press).

Science Confirms Reconnective Healing

4.
Dr. Konstantin Korotkov
Reconnective Healing Electrophotonic Experiments 2008 - 2011

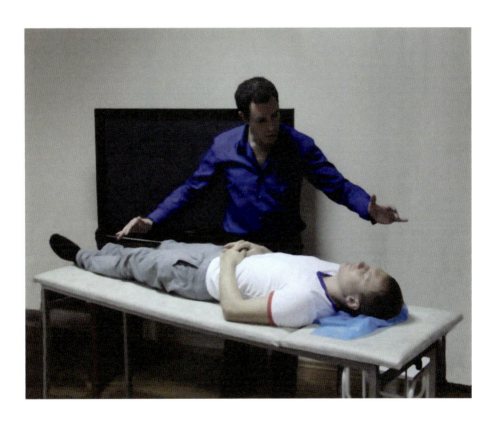

In this chapter we use the following abbreviations:

1L, 2L.....5L and 1R......5R fingers of the left and right hands, correspondingly, beginning from thumb to little finger.	
EF F somatic state of a person.	Energy Field with filter. Related to the
EF wF emotional state of a person	Energy Field without filter. Related to the
EPC	Electrophotonic Capture.
EPI	Electrophotonic Imaging.
EPI/GDV Camera Pro or EPI/GDV Compact -	EPI Instruments.
GDV	Gas Discharge Visualization.

During the Reconnective workshop two types of measurements have been conducted:

1) Measuring of participants' energy with EPC instrument (www.ktispb.ru) before and after the workshop.

2) Monitoring of Space during the workshop with the Electrophotonic Sensor. (www.korotkov.org).

5. EPC/GDV Technique
(www.korotkov.org; www.ktispb.ru)

Electrophotonic is a promising direction in the construction of new non-invasive automatic procedures that assess the body's condition during minimum interventions into vital functions. The diagnosis of predisposition to some diseases, the choice of the most adequate treatment policy and the monitoring of human bioresponses to various environmental factors are important aspects in preventive health care services. Electrophotonic method investigates human functional states, by assessing electro-optical parameters of the skin that are based on the registration of physical processes emerging from electron components of tissue conductivity. This technique allows one to capture the image of Electrophotonic impulse around human fingertips and extract information about sympathetic and parasympathetic activities. The quantitative difference in parameters between two systems, which is equal to autonomic tone, and called activation coefficient can be used as the indirect measure for cognitive function. Integral area of Electrophotonic impulse is a presentation of calculated fractality level and consistency of the captured image. Integral entropy calculated as a Shennon information entropy[i] is a measure of the deviation from the functional physiological and psycho emotional balance. Thus, Electrophotonic approach can then be used as a model to bridge the gaps in health disparities by creating an innovative approach to address health aspects in real time measurements, which will improve rural health outcomes.

The EPC/GDV camera is presently the state-of-the-art in bioelectrography[ii]. It utilizes a high frequency (1024 Hz), high-voltage (10 kV) input to the finger (or other object to be measured), which is placed on the electrified glass lens of the EPC camera. Because the electrical current applied to the body is very low, most human subjects do not experience any sensation when exposing their fingertip to the camera. In practice, the applied electric field is pulsed on and off every 10 microseconds, and the fingertip is exposed for only 0.5 seconds. This causes a corona discharge of light-emitting plasma to stream outward from the fingertip. The light emitted from the finger is detected directly by a CCD (charge-coupled detector), which is the state-of-the-art in scientific instruments such as telescopes to measure extremely low-level light. The signal from the CCD is sent directly to a computer, and software analysis is done to calculate a variety of parameters that characterize the pattern of light emitted, including brightness, total area, fractality, and density. The software can also provide color enhancement to enable subtle features such as intensity variations of the image to be perceived. The underlying principle of camera operation is similar to the well-known Kirlian effect[iii] but modern technology allows reproducible stable data with quantitative computer analysis. Purposeful investigations allowed the discovery of the parameters that are optimal from the point of obtaining critical information on the biological object's state with the minimum of invasiveness. These findings are described in more than 200 research works in the international scientific literature, 15 patents, 7 books in English, French, German, Italian, Russian, and Spanish.

This biophysical concept of the principles of GDV measurements is based on the ideas of quantum biophysics[iv]. This is a further development of well-known ideas of A. Szent-Györgyi concerning the transfer of electron-excited states along the chains of molecular protein complexes. The EPC technique measures the level of functional energy stored by the particular systems of an organism. This level is defined by the power of the electron-excited states and the character of their transport along the chains of albumin molecules. The level of functional energy is correlated with health status, but it is only one of many of the components that define health. It works together with genetic predisposition, psycho-emotional states, environmental loading (food, water, air, ecology) and other factors. This approach may be associated with the oriental notion of the energy transfer along meridians.

EPC/GDV bioelectrographic systems have had practical applications in the several main areas, such as medicine[v,vi,vii], sport[viii], study of liquids[ix], water[x] and materials[xi].

Science Confirms Reconnective Healing

In assessing human subjects, the EPC-grams (emission patterns after computer processing) of all ten fingers are made and analyzed. All 10 EPC-grams from the fingers then undergo analysis via another software program creating the model of Energy Field around the body and the diagrams showing the energy distribution in the various organ systems. This is based on the map correlating the human fingers with different systems and organs of the body in accordance with Traditional Chinese Medicine (TCM) approach [i].

The variance in the reproducibility of the GDV patterns of emission and the calculated diagrams is about 10% for human fingers, and about 3% for materials[xii]. The 2-3% variability pertaining to materials testing is considered to be random error. However, the 10% variation with respect to human fingers reflects not only standard error, but the fluctuations in the energy dynamics of a living being, i.e., the "flicker of the flame of life." As it is shown in numerous studies, the pattern of emission, which determines the relative energy distribution in the person's organs, remains constant from day to day. That is, each adult displays an "energy pattern signature" in this method of testing.

Scientific research in GDV carried out in medicine revealed correlations of GDV parameters with other measurable characteristics of the organism[xiii]. Several correlations have been found: first of all, with age; with the level of blood pressure and blood formula; with cardio variability indices, and others. Reliable statistical differences of GDV parameters of groups of healthy individuals and groups of patients with various nosologies have been observed.

Electrophotonic Sensor for remote detecting human emotions

New "Electrophotonic Sensor" has been developed based on EPC technology which allows to record the changes of the environmental parameters in the process of natural events such as sunset, sunrise or sun eclipse. At the same time Sensor parameters change under the influence of human emotions or musical performance. Measurements conducted during religious ceremonies, yoga meditations, public lectures, musical performances demonstrated that the signal of the Sensor statistically significantly changes during measurements and these changes are correlated with the course of event[xiv].

For calibration the EPC/GDV instrument we are using titanium cylinder 15 mm (0.6 inch) in diameter connected to the grounding jack of the instrument. (Titanium is very stable and does not oxidize in gaseous discharge). The principle of the EPI/GDV instrument was being used in the "Electrophotonic Sensor". The principles of operations are as follows (fig.1).

For detection emotions cylinder 1 is connected to the special antenna 2 designed to create non-homogenous electromagnetic field. Generator 3 produces impulses of voltage 7 kV amplitude, 10 mcs duration, coming with 1 kHz frequency in 0.5 s packs every 5 s. Voltage is applied to the transparent conductive layer 4 on the quartz electrode 5. Due to the bias current from antenna 2 a gaseous discharge 7 between cylinder 1 and electrode 5 is generated. The glow of the discharge is detected by a special TV system 6 and after digitizing is kept as series of image files on a memory stick 8 connected to the instrument. Instrument runs on 12 V rechargeable batteries 9 for more than 100 hours in automatic mode. Files are kept in memory with time marks, which allows correlate parameters after data processing with time sequence of the events under study.

From physical point of view this device measures changes in the first Townsend air ionization coefficient as a function of environmental changes. At the same time bias current in the electrical chain depends on the capacitance of space between antenna 2 and electroconductive subjects around.

Emotions are related to the activity of the parasympathetic division of the autonomic nervous system, which changes blood microcirculation, perspiration, sweating, and other functions of the body, resulting in the changes of the overall conductivity of the body and the conductivity of acupuncture points in particular. So the presence in the vicinity of the instrument of the emotional people may change the conductivity of space and, hence, the signal of the sensor. At the same time in laboratory conditions at night without presence of people variability of data during 6 hours was at the level 0.5 – 1%. Before the measurement instrument should be "warmed up" by operating for 30-50 minutes with cylinder connected to the grounding jack of the instrument.

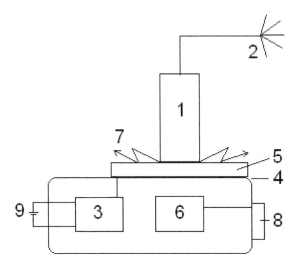

Fig.5.1. The schematic design of the "Electrophotonic Sensor". 1 – titanium cylinder; 2 - special antenna; 3 - impulses generator; 4 - transparent conductive layer; 5 - quartz electrode; 6 - TV system; 7 - gaseous discharge; 8 - memory stick; 9 - 12 V rechargeable batteries.

6. EXPERIMENTAL RESULTS

DATA OF PARTICIPANTS ENERGY FIELD

Participant were measured in 2008-2009 during several Reconnective sessions before and after the workshop. Several groups of participants were selected:

Newcomers;

Experienced practitioners;

Trainers;

Top-level trainers.

Data was processed in several modes.

Percentage of changes for the parameters was calculated in accordance with a formula:

$$(S_{after} - S_{initial})/S_{initial} * 100\%$$

Area is associated with the power of human average Energy Field.

Los Angeles (USA) September 13, 14, 2008.

23 people took part in the study, 16 women and 7 men, age 32 +/- 10.

Averaged %% of changes in the Energy Field in the group of 23 people was 17%. About 14% of people had positive changes from 10% to 50%, 10% of people had positive changes less than 10%, and 76% of people had no changes in the Area of their Energy Field.

St. Petersburg (Russia) September 15, 16, 2009.

Reconnective Healing workshop by Eric Pearl and Instructor took place in St. Petersburg, Russia September 15 and 16. Nine people took part in the workshop (1 woman and 8 men, age 18 – 41). All participants had no idea about Reconnective Healing before.

Processing demonstrated statistically significant increase and balance of Energy Field for the group with 95% probability. Fig.6-1 present results of averaged on the group data, while fig.6-2 demonstrate data for all participants.

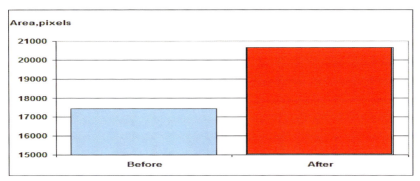

Fig. 6.1. Area of Energy Field before and after the workshop averaged on the group of 9 people.

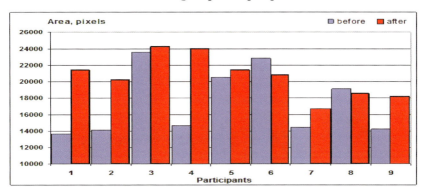

Fig. 6.2. Area of Energy Field before and after the workshop for all participants.

Los Angeles (USA), September – October 2009

Results are presented depending on the participants' category.

Advanced Practitioners

9 people took part in the study in the first day and 12 people in the second day, 7 women and 5 men, age 32 +/- 10.

Results of Energy Field measurements during two days are presented at Fig.6-3 and 6-4.

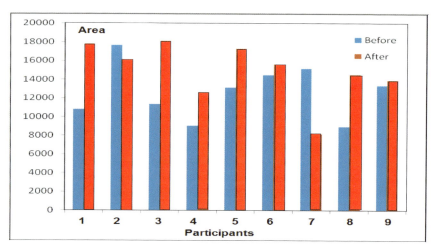

Fig 6.3. EF for Advanced Practitioners before and after session in the first day.

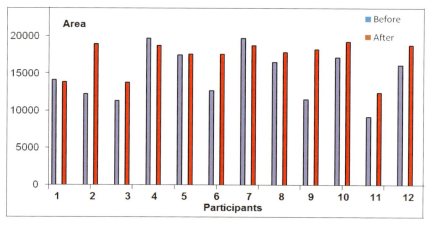

Fig 6.4. EF for Advanced Practitioners before and after session in the second day.

Science Confirms Reconnective Healing

As we see from the graphs in the first day:

for 7 people EF increased;

for 2 people EF decreased;

and in the second day:

for 8 people EF increased;

for 2 people EF had no changes;

for 2 people EF decreased;

For the first day this increase was statistically significant with $p < 0.05$.

Instructors

3 people took part in the study, 2 women and 1 man, age 32 +/- 10.

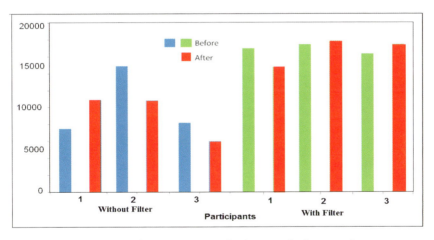

Fig 6.5 EF for Instructors before and after session.

In this case data were collected with and without special plastic membrane, which allows distinguish between psychological and somatic EF. This membrane (or filter) is placed on the surface of glass electrode where we place fingers. This allows to avoid the influence of skin perspiration to the discharge development. For 1 person EF

57

Science Confirms Reconnective Healing

increased, for 2 people decreased, while we need to mention slight increase of somatic EF for 2 people (green bars).

Practitioners Mentors

10 people took part in the study, 5 women and 5 men, age 32 +/- 10.

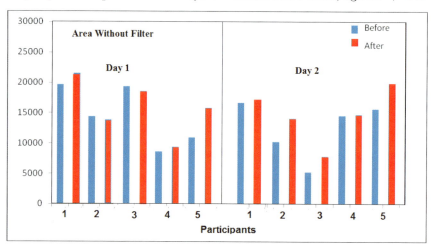

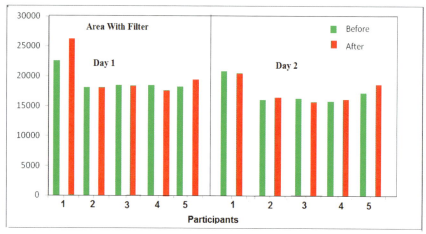

Fig 6.6. EF for Practitioners Mentors before and after session in the first and second day.

As we see from the graphs for 7 people EF increased and for 3 people it was practically no changes.

Science Confirms Reconnective Healing

Amsterdam, Holland, November 12 - 17, 2009

Measurements protocol

Three types of GDV/EPC measurements has been established during the seminar:

1. Influence of attending the practical seminar.
2. Influence of Reconnective Healing session.
3. Influence of selfhealing session on advanced practitioners.

Participants of the workshop

40 people (27 women and 13 men, age from 18 to 61) from the participants of the practical seminar took part in GDV/EPC measurements. They were asked to come for EPC screening before the seminar (12-13 November) and then after the seminar (16-17 November). Each person has two captures made with filter and without filter.

Participants of this type of EPC measurements were coming for screening all day long (with 15 minutes interval).

Reconnective healing session

12 people (7 women and 7 men, age from 21 to 43) took part in this type of EPC measurements.

They were measured before the Reconnective Healing session and right after it.

This research was made in the evening at 9-11 pm, November 12.

Selfhealing session of advanced practitioners

13 advanced practitioners (7 women and 6 men, age from 21 to 53) took part in this type of measurements.

They were measured right before the selfhealing session and right after it before the dinner on November 16.

Data processing

59

Science Confirms Reconnective Healing

Two types of data processing for these types of measurements were applied:

1. Processing in GDV/EPC software – "GDV Energy Field".
2. Advanced processing of all data in special software "GDV Scientific laboratory".

In the second case more deep, advanced and complex calculations after processing in GDV/EPC software using Microsoft Office Excel program were made.

Summary

Participants of the workshop (40 people)

We should notice that almost all people that took part in this type of measurements were very tired at the first screening (before the seminar) and at the second (after the seminar) too. Their tiredness before the seminar during EPC capture can be explained by the fact that they appeared right from airplanes or after a long ride by car. After the seminar they were tired because seminar ended very late each day during weekend, so participants didn't have enough sleep.

That is why we can't see statistically significant difference in their physiological or psycho-emotional state.

Most of participants demonstrated non-significant changes in psycho-emotional state (below 10% deviation - natural fluctuation of human state) 16 from 40 people showed overall harmonization of their state – decrease in Form coefficient. 13 people showed increase in Form coefficient) and almost no shift in Area (2 positive and 1 negative) and Average intensity (100% of participants demonstrated no shift).. Big shifts in this parameter can be explained by the influence of Reconnective frequencies. Decrease means calming down of psycho-emotional state and harmonization, and big increase means excitation that can be explained as activation of some processes in the human body.

If we take into consideration the absence of significant shifts in Area and Average intensity of energy field we may attribute shifts in Form Coefficient to the redistribution of energy.

Reconnective Healing session (12 people)

On physiological level participants didn't show any changes in their state (100% of participants). We know that physiological state doesn't change fast and during the time of healing session (less than 1 hour) no significant changes took place.

On psycho-emotional level we can see shift in Form coefficient parameter for 9 from 12 (75%) of participants. And no significant changes in other parameters.

This shift is connected, as we have mentioned earlier, with overall harmonization of human energy field.

Selfhealing session of advanced practitioners (13 people)

We should take into consideration that advanced practitioners were also very tired after a very difficult weekend and a lack of sleep. But there were shifts in Form coefficient for 7 people on psycho-emotional level and for 6 people on physiological level. From the other hand big difference of these results from results of US workshops may be an indication of different attitude to the training process between European and American population. This topic needs more detailed study.

Conclusion

We may conclude that Reconnective Healing sessions in Amsterdam resulted in changes of human energy field: harmonization and redistribution of human energy.

Data processing in "GDV Energy Field" program

Data for this type of study was processed in "GDV Energy Field" program and assessed in Microsoft Office Excel program. On diagrams average values for the group are presented. Increase in Area may be correlated with the overall increase of energy output, while decrease of entropy is related to the harmonization of the condition.

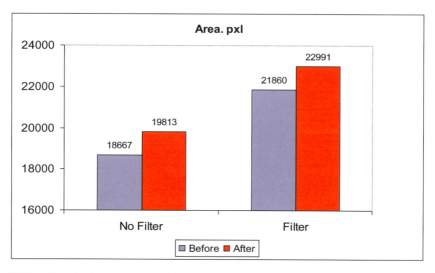

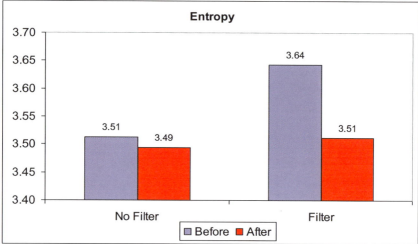

Fig.6.7. Changes of Area and Entropy before and after workshop.

Science Confirms Reconnective Healing

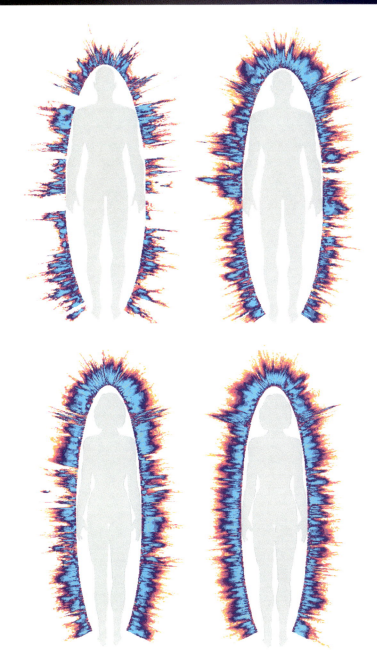

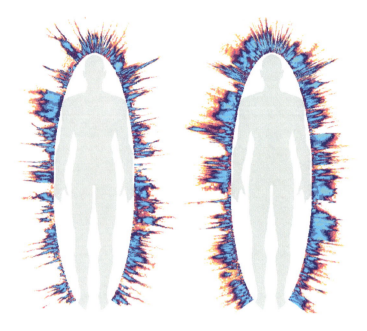

Fig 6.8. Examples of Energy Fields before and after the workshop.

DISCUSSION

Analysis of all data is presented in Table 6.1.

Table 6.1. Changes of Area/Form Coefficient of Psychological EF (without filter).

Place, year	Session type	Increase	No Changes	Decrease	Total N of people
LA 2008	Workshop	6/2	17/6	0/15	23
St Petersburg 2009	Training	7/2	0/0	2/7	9
LA 2009	AP 1	7/5	0/4	2/0	9
	AP 2	8/1	2/11	2/0	12
	Instructors	1/2	0/1	2/0	3
	Mentors	7/1	3/8	0/1	10
	Healing session	0/0	12/3	0/9	12
	Self-healing	1/0	10/6	2/7	13
	Total	37	44	10	91

Area is associated with the power of EF, so increase in Area we may be considered as positive outcome of the session.

Form Coefficient (FC) is the measure of harmonization of EF, so decrease in Form Coefficient may be considered as positive outcome of the session.

We can make several mail conclusions from these data:

1. Two types of positive effects for participants during Reconnective Healing sessions were recorded: increase in Area and decrease in Form Coefficient. In most cases either one effect or another was recorded.

2. At some sessions Area of EF was increasing for most of the participants (St Petersburg and LA 2009); while in LA 2008 session it was practically no changes of Area, but very significant changes of the Form Coefficient.

3. Abovementioned effects may be related to different modalities of Reconnective Healing, conveyed by different trainers.

4. No difference between women and men responses was found.

5. Results strongly depend on the trainer: strong effects were recorded at some sessions, and practically no effects at the other.

6. Response to Reconnective Healing is very individual and may depend on the initial condition of a person: the level of stress, tiredness, psycho-physiological condition.

7. Very little changes of somatic EF (with membrane - filter) was found. So we may conclude that Reconnective Healing had no negative effects to physiological conditions. From our experience we know that positive effects may be expected after several days after the session.

8. For European population strong effects of EF harmonization were found, but we do not know to which factors this may be attributed.

9. More experiments are needed with detailed control of all factors.

DATA OF ELECTROPHOTONIC SENSOR

Two types of Electrophotonic Sensors were being used during the conference: antenna type and "Sputnik" type. Antenna sensor was operated from computer and powered from wall outlet, while "Sputnik" sensor ran on battery in automatic mode without connection to the computer. Information was recorded on a memory steak. After finishing recording information was processed in "Scientific Lab" program (producer KTI Co, St. Petersburg, Russia).

All the experiments were conducted in double-blind regime.

Los Angeles, September 18-20, 2008

Monitoring of Space with the "Antenna" type sensor was conducted every Conference day by Krishna Madappa. Data processing was done by Dr. Konstantin Korotkov. Sensor was positioned in the conference room and connected to the EPC Camera and to the notebook computer. All devices were warmed up for 1 hour before the arriving of the participants, and measurements were half an hour before the conference and during all the day of the conference. Processing of data was done in "GDV SciLab" program. Graphs below demonstrate time dynamics of the Electrophotonic Sensor parameters for every day with marked moments of interest.

SEPTEMBER 18

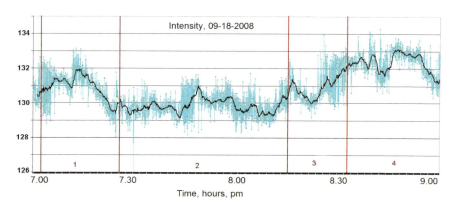

Fig.6.9. Time variations of Intensity recorded by "Antenna" type sensor.

     18.30 -19.04   Room set up process, **Dr. Emoto** enters room.

1. 19.05 -19.23   **Instructor** initiates welcome address & inaugurates conf. Hopi elder, Vernon conveys prayer and blessing.

2. 19.24- 20.20   **Instructor intro. Dr. Emoto**, who speaks in Japanese with the aid of a translator. Plays music

3. 20.21- 20.30   **Emoto San** Jokes and laughter opera composition by "Maria Callas" while with the attendees sing on.

4. 20.35 -21.09   Continues talk on consciousness and water, a song and then concludes.

As wee see from the graphs, **09/18** was very clear reaction to the beginning of presentations by Instructor DeVita and active reactions during all the day. Reactions were presented both on Area and Intensity graphs. Both Area and Intensity had some increase during the day. **09/19** we may define reaction to the beginning of the presentation (1), later on the day no specific reactions could be defined. Intensity was increasing during all the day.

Science Confirms Reconnective Healing

SEPTEMBER 19

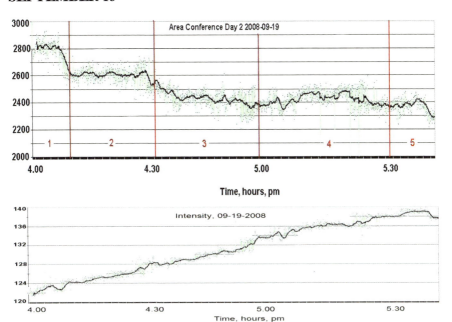

Fig.6.10. Time variations of Area and Intensity recorded by "Antenna" type sensor.

Time sequence regime of activity :

1	16.00 -16.09	**Instructor** begins and leads the attendees into RC process and intro. the works of Dr's. Schwartz, Tiller and Korotkov
2	16.10 - 16.31	**Eric** arrives and sets up to play chanelling recordings from 1995. and 1999.
3	16.32 - 17.05	Eric's guidance and advice to attendees as follows.
4	17.06 - 17.40	**Eric's** discussions. 1718 **Instructor** final thoughts.
5	17.30	Session concludes. Data capture continues till 1740.

SEPTEMBER 20

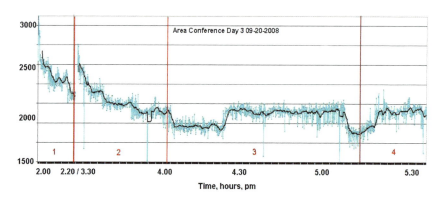

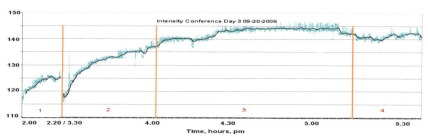

Fig. 6.11. Time variations of Area and Intensity recorded by "Antenna" type sensor.

Time sequence regime of activity:

1   14.00 - 15.31   **Instructor** on podium & introduces **Dr. Gary Schwartz**. Schwartz outlines the sum content of the presentation. (Due to technical problems recording was interrupted at 2.20 pm).

2   15.31 - 15.58   Intermission

3   15.59 - 17.15   **Dr. Bill Tillers** lecture

4   17.15 - 17.36   **Instructor** asked to reference on reciprocal space and it's implications especially during healing.

SEPTEMBER 21

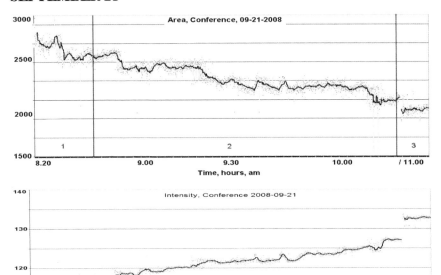

Fig. 6.12. Time variations of Area and Intensity recorded by "Antenna" type sensor.

<u>Time sequence regime of activity</u> :

1	08.21 - 08.36	Steven Halpern's composition of "OM"
2	08.37 - 09.41	Dr. Korotkov arrives and begins presentation
	10.24 - 11.04	Recess
3	11.05 - 12.35	Panel Discussion

Science Confirms Reconnective Healing

Los Angeles, September – October 2009

Two types of Eco-Sensor were being used during the conference: antenna type at September 25, 26 and 27 and "Sputnik" type October 03 and 04. Antenna sensor was operated from computer and powered from wall outlet, while "Sputnik" sensor ran on battery in automatic mode without connection to the computer. Information was recorded on a memory steak.

In all cases sensor was positioned in the corner of the room at the table without chance of shaking or moving the table. Temperature and humidity in the room was controlled and stayed in normal range.

Graphs presented below demonstrate reaction of the sensor to the entropy in the auditorium.

Summary

Workshop September 25-27.

High variation of parameters were recorded during workshop.

The highest response was recorded on Sept 26 by all parameters.

Yoga class Oct 3.

Increase of Area and Intensity after the beginning of yoga session was recorded. During the class parameters were quite stable.

Conference Oct 4_1.

Very high reaction to the presentation of Dr Korotkov was recorded for all parameters. During presentation of Dr Tiller parameters were quite stable.

Conference Oct 4_2.

Increase of Area and Entropy and decrease of Intensity after beginning of Dr Sigafoose presentation was recorded. Stable level of signal was kept during brake time. Presentation of Instructor was reflected by high variation of all parameters followed by short closing words by Dr Pearl.

Science Confirms Reconnective Healing

Workshop 25 September 2009

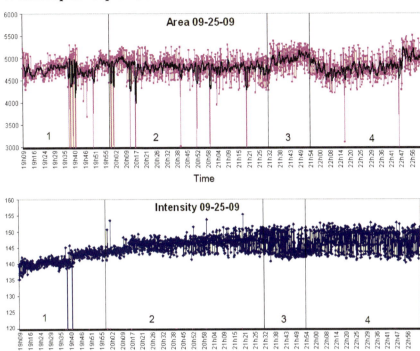

Fig.6.13. Time variations of Area and Intensity and recorded by "Antenna" type sensor.

Time sequence regime of activity :

1	19.09 - 19.59	**Instructor** on podium "Essence Lecture" and then introduces RCA's.
2	20.00 - 21.32	**Eric** conveys insights/jokes & discussions. 2035 , engages attendees who have restricted hand motion.
3		Recess
4	21.54 - 22.57	Eric on podium with attendees now in direct participation of RC. Concludes day 1 with this affirmation - "We are Light."

Science Confirms Reconnective Healing

Workshop 26 September 2009

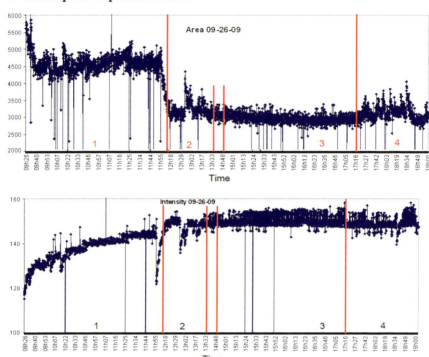

Fig.6.14. Time variations of Area and Intensity recorded by "Antenna" type sensor.

Time sequence regime of activity :

1 09.26 – 12.15   Attendees settling in & **Instructor** invigorates the group. Instructor proceeds to convey the essence

2 12.16 – 13.35   Instructor conveys studies done on influencing leaf 1223 , Eric arrives/   1336 – 1447   Lunch

3 14.48 – 16.51   **Eric** arrives & assays strength of presence in all participants

4 17.16 – 19.03   **Eric & Instructor** conveying "Hands Behind Back" process 1757 Session concludes

Workshop 27 September 2009

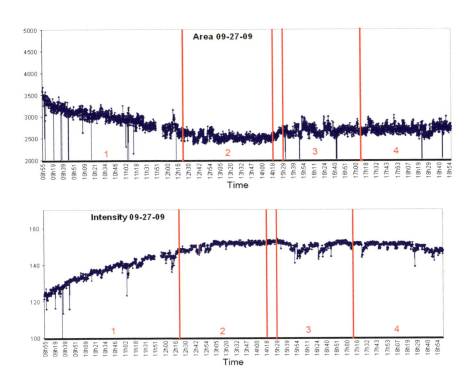

Fig.6.15. Time variations of Area and Intensity recorded by "Antenna" type sensor.

<u>Time sequence regime of activity</u> :

1   08.55 - 12.23   Attendees arriving, high buzz from room till 0935 . **Instructor** arrives
2   12.24 - 14.28   **Eric** arrives
    14.28 - 15.27   Lunch
3   15.30 - 17.10   **Eric** arrives & continues to elaborate,
4   17.13 - 18.50   **Eric** Hologram healing! 1842 , Session concludes

Science Confirms Reconnective Healing

Yoga session 03 October (fig.17)

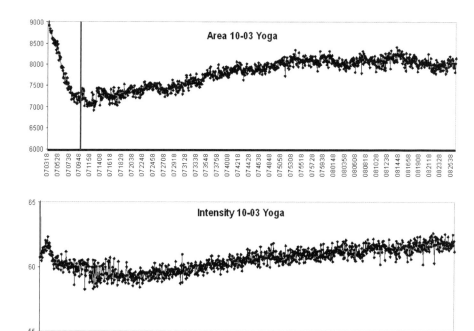

Fig.6.16. Time variations of Area and Intensity and recorded by "Sputnik" type sensor.

Increase of Area and Intensity after the beginning of yoga session was recorded. During the class parameters were quite stable.

Conference 04 October

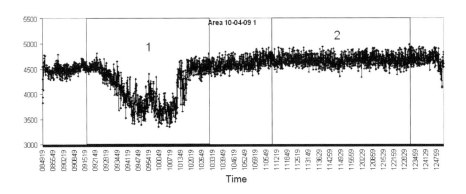

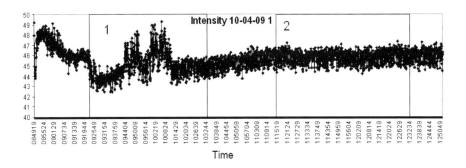

Fig.6.17. Time variations of Area and Intensity recorded by "Sputnik" type sensor.

Very high reaction to the presentation of **Dr Korotkov** (area 1 at the graphs) was recorded for all parameters. During presentation of **Dr Tiller** (area 2 at the graphs) parameters were quite stable.

Science Confirms Reconnective Healing

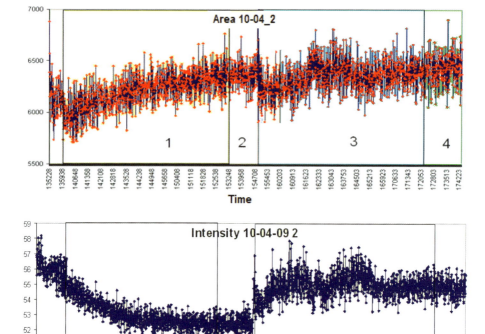

Fig.6.18. Time variations of Area and Intensity recorded by "Sputnik" type sensor.

<u>Time sequence regime of activity</u> :

1   14.05-15.30   Dr Sigafoose presentation

2   15.30-15.50   Lunch

3   15.50-17.28   Presentation of Instructor

4   17.28   short closing words by Dr Pearl

Amsterdam, November 13 - 15 2009

In these sessions Two types of devices were used:
1. "GDV Compact" EPC camera with standard antenna type sensor.
2. "GDV Eco-Tester" with "Sputnik" type sensor.

November 13

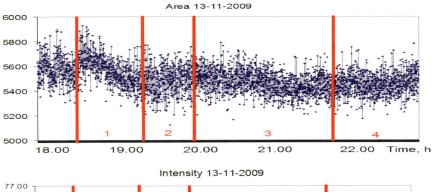

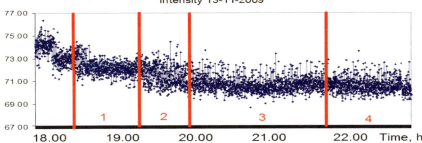

Fig.6.19. Time variations of Area and Intensity recorded by "Antenna" type sensor.

Time sequence regime of activity :

1.	18:20	People entering the room.
2.	19:10	Instructor speaking.
3.	19:48	Eric on the stage.
4.	21:40	Instructor speaking.

79

14th November

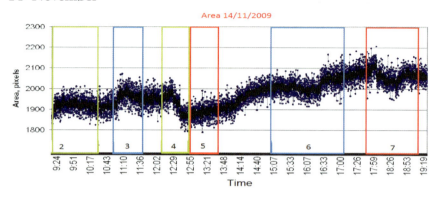

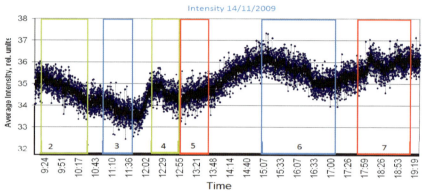

Fig.6.20. Time variations of Area and Intensity recorded by "Sputnik" type sensor.

Time sequence regime of activity :

1 8:30   People entering the room.
2 9:05   Instructor on the stage.
3 10:46   People going to tables. Healing exercises.
4 12:04   Instructor.
5 12:50   Eric. 13:30 Lunch
6 15:00   Healing stories from TA's.
7 17:35   Eric. 19:08 People leaving the room

15th November

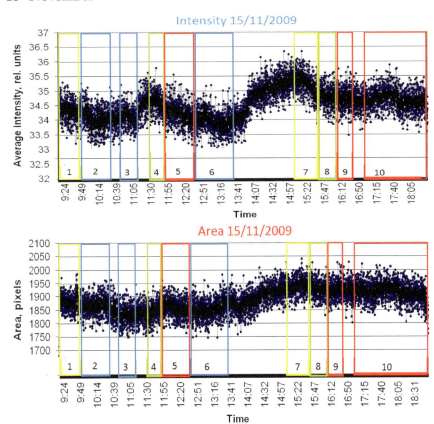

Fig.6.21. Time variations of Area and Intensity recorded by "Sputnik" type sensor.

Time sequence regime of activity :

	8:33	People filling the room.
1	9:00	Different speakers on stage.
2	9:48	People going to tables.
3	10:48	Exercises.
4	11:31	Instructor speaking.
5	11:53	Eric speaking.

6	12:39	People going to tables. Exercises.
7	15:05	Kelly speaking.
8	15:32	Instructor speaking.
9	15:45	Eric speaking.
10		Eric speaking. 18:44 People leaving the room.

As we see from the graphs, most of significant moments in different days of the sessions were reflected on the graphs. This may be presented as increase of parameters or separate peaks.

15/11 after presentation of Instructor and Eric reaction to exercises was in decreasing of Intensity graph (area 6). We may conclude that after long session people were tired and subsequent break was reflected as increase in parameters.

Strong shifts on the presented diagrams were connected with presence or absence of people in the room (during lunch or break).

Because of very huge room all the influences were very weak and sensors registered influences, but shifts (connected with Reconnective Healing exercises) were small in comparison with previous measurements.

For example, only Eco-tester has registered the appearance of Eric Pearl on the stage on Friday evening 13/11 – shift in Average intensity parameter (19:48) was registered.

Sedona, December 4 – 6, 2009

December 4

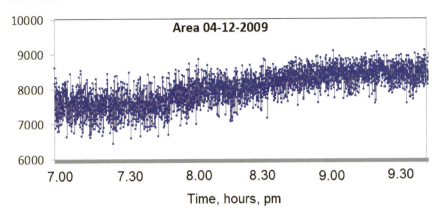

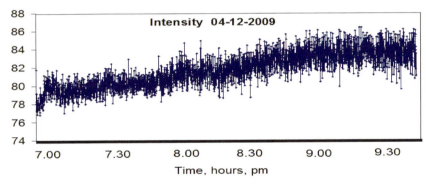

Fig.6.22. Time variations of Area and Intensity recorded by "Antenna" type sensor.

1858: Sensor activated. The seminar room was being prepared for the following day. RCP (Practitioners) + RCM (mentors) were arranging the space from Podium setting to ATD (Attendee) seating to MTB (Mass. table bay) positioning. Volunteers for the seminar were also present in the set up process. Seating set up to accommodate 100 + participants.

2131: Sensor cycle concluded.

During workshop we see high increase both of Area and Intensity. After the end of workshop signal became stable.

Science Confirms Reconnective Healing

December 5

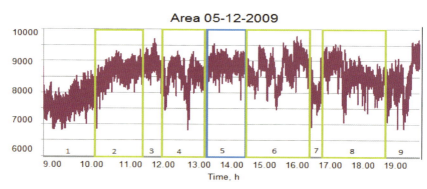

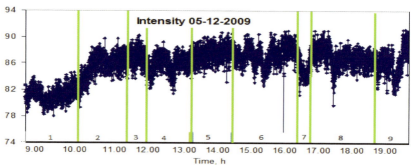

Fig.23. Time variations of Area and Intensity recorded by "Antenna" type sensor.

Time sequence regime of activity :
1. 08.36-11.23   **Instructor**
2. 09.50-11.22   **Instructor**
3. 11.24 - 11.43   Recess
4. 11.44 - 12.53   **Instructor** TA's on basics of table etiquette
5. 12.54 - 14.15   RCH sessions in progress in seminar room
6. 14.16 - 15.58   practical processes
7. 15.59 - 16.21   Recess
8. 16.22 - 18.25   Q & A & RC w animals
9. 18.26 - 19.20   Session concludes at 1825

December 6

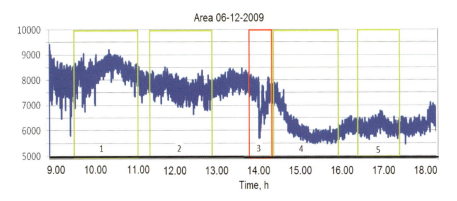

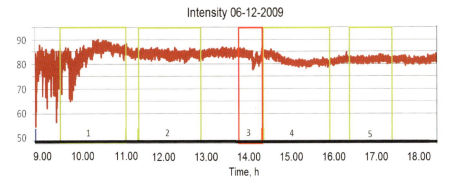

Fig.6.24. Time variations of Area and Intensity recorded by "Antenna" type sensor.

Time sequence regime of activity :

1   08.57-11.00   **Instructor** opens the day
2   11.08 - 11.25 Recess
3   11.25 - 12.53 Instructor conveys results of survey + personal process.
4   13.50 -14.11   Instructor w a few RCP's did a RCF initiation to bottled water so as to raise the pH
5   14.11 - 15.59 RCPractice conveyed by Instructor
6   16.25 - 17.36 Instructor w session insights to ATD's; concludes w closed eye meditation. Seminar concludes!

Science Confirms Reconnective Healing

Twentieth Annual ISSSEEM Conference

Introduction

During the XXth Annual ISSSEEM Conference in July 2010 a lot of presentations have devoted to different modalities of healing. This topic is of importance both for the practice of CAM and for understanding the mechanisms of consciousness. In the scope of the conference a full-day workshop "Real-Time Measurements of the Human Energy Field: Quantifying Subtle Energies with the Electrophotonic Imaging based on Gas Discharge Visualization Technique" was held. During workshop a series experiments were conducted based on Reconnective Healing modalities. Herewith we are presenting results of theses experiments.

Dr Len Wisneski, Dr Berney Williams, Dr Konstantin Korotkov and Krishna Madappa conducted the experiments; Instructor was organizing the Reconnection Healing process.

Participants

More than 50 people of both genders presented at the workshop and participated in experiments. All details of the experiments were clearly presented to people. For some experiments volunteers were selected.

Process of the experiments

    1.   Instructor introduced The Reconnective Healing technique to all participants.

    2.   Instructor and his assistant facilitated Reconnective Healing to 5 volunteers. People were measured with EPC before and after treatment.

    3.   All participants meditated sending intentions to water measured with EPC before and after.

    4.   "EPC Sputnik" sensor was recording in an automatic mode for several hours after the lunch.

Science Confirms Reconnective Healing

Results

The Reconnective Healing

All 10 EPC-grams of fingers of participants were processed before and after healing. Fig.26 presents results of ANOVA statistical processing of the Area parameter. As we see from the graphs for all participants' energy increase was recorded, while for 3 people changes were statistically significant. Similar changes in the Entropy parameter signified significant harmonization of the participants' condition. Fig.27 presents an example of the Energy Field changes for one of the participants before and after the Reconnective Healing.

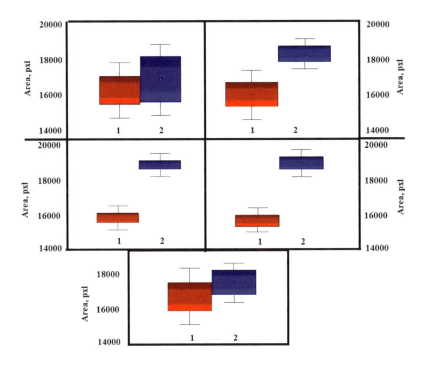

Fig.6.25. ANOVA statistical processing of the Area parameter for 5 people before (1) and after (2) Reconnective Healing.

87

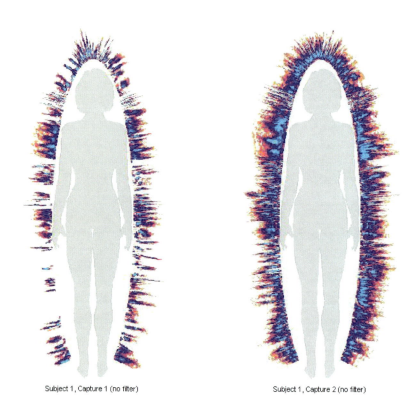

Fig.6.26. EF of the participant before and after the Reconnective Healing.

Electrophotonic sensor "Sputnik"

Sensor was positioned in the corner of the room and turned on at the beginning of the lunch break. Sensor was a stand-alone device battery operated, signal was recorded every 5 seconds in automatic mode and saved on a memory card. Every recorded point had a time mark. After finishing the workshop all data were loaded into computer and processed in the "GDV SciLab" program where time dynamics of several parameters have been calculated. Time line of Sputnik parameters are presented at fig.27.

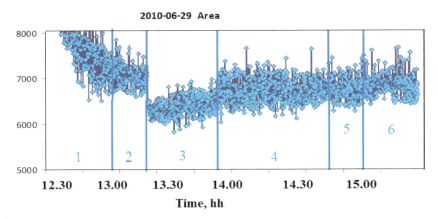

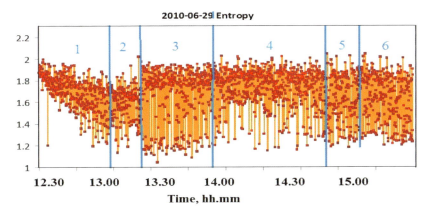

Fig.6.27. Time dynamics of "Sputnik" sensor Area and Entropy parameters during the workshop.

Different moments of the workshop are marked as follows:
1. Lunch break.
2. Beginning of the workshop.
3. Instructor introduced Reconnective Healing.
4. Workshop in progress.
5. Meditation on water.

As we see from the graphs, at the moment when Instructor was introducing the Reconnective Healing and trained people in feeling energy, the highest reaction was recorded. The difference of parameters both from the previous and subsequent time dynamics was statistically significant. Meditation on water significantly changed variation of the entropy parameter compared with the previous time which was kept during the Dee-Gee-Doo treatment till the end of the workshop.

Riccione, Italy, 12-14 November 2010-11-21

All measurements were done with "Sputnik" sensor connected to the GDV Compact instrument.

Sensor was positioned at the back of the hall.

November 12 morning

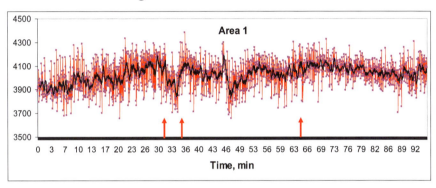

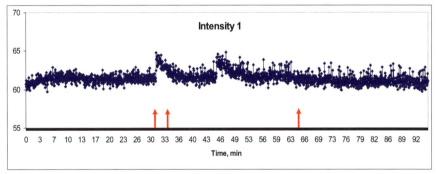

Fig.6.28. Presentation of Instructor

0-30 min background without people in the hall.

31 min – people in the hall, beginning of Instructor presentation.

65 min – beginning of exercises.

These moments reflected at the Area, Intensity and Inner noise. No reactions at Entropy.

At this conference overall reactions of the instrument was less compared with previous US measurements. This may depend on the size of the hall, position of the sensor, reaction of public.

More data should be collected for the conclusions.

DISCUSSION

We had 15 sessions with Electrophotonic Sensor at the Reconnective events: 7 during conferences and 8 during workshops. At all sessions Sensor responded to significant events in the room, in most cases during presentations of Eric or Instructor. At the same time behavior of the graphs was different in different sessions. We may define the following moments:

1. Area graphs had both ascending and descending response. We pay attention that numbers at the graphs are different due to using sensor elements of different construction. Finely the most sensitive "Sputnik" sensor was developed.

2. Area variations have been changing from 11% to 100% in different sessions (Table 7).

3. Recording lasted from 1h40 to 10h30. The level of variations did not depend on the length of a session.

4. During the conferences only some presenters stimulated the reaction of the sensor.

5. Control recordings in the laboratory without presence of people demonstrated variations of Area and Intensity at the level 3-7% without any specific moments (see examples below at fig.29).

6. Measurements in Amsterdam (11-2009) demonstrated less variations of a signal compared with measurements in the USA. The reason may be very big size of the auditorium where workshops took place.

7. Measurements taken with two independent sensors in parallel demonstrated very high consistency in recording significant events during workshop:

11/13/2009 Decrease of Area in segment 1 of both graphs; Increase of Area in the beginning of segment 4 of both graphs.

Science Confirms Reconnective Healing

11/14/2009 Similar type of Area curves in segments 2 and 3 of both graphs; Increase of Area in segments 5-6 of both graphs; Increase of Intensity in segment 5 and 6 of both graphs.

11/15/2009 Increase of Area in segment 7 of both graphs; Increase of Intensity in segments 3, 4 and 7 of both graphs.

All abovementioned features demonstrate that recorded variations of a Sensor signal was not just random, but were related to events in the room. They may be related both to the activity of the presenter and to the reaction of the audience.

From all the data we can make the conclusion that during sessions of Reconnective Healing structurization of a space in the auditorium takes place. The physical background of this effect needs attention and further investigation.

Science Confirms Reconnective Healing

Table 6.2. Changes of Sensor parameters during sessions

Date, mmddyy	Type of event	Length of the session	Area changes
918-2008	Conference	2h30	29%
919-2008	Conference	1h40	40%
920-2008	Conference	3h30	67%
921-2008	Conference	4h00	33%
925-2009	Workshop	4h00	59%
926-2009	Workshop	9h30	100%
927-2009	Workshop	10h00	55%
1003-2009	Workshop	1h20	25%
1004-2009-1	Conference	4h00	35%
1004-2009-2	Conference	3h30	16%
1113-2009-1*	Workshop	8h10	14%
1113-2009-2*	Workshop	8h10	13%
1114-2009-1*	Workshop	9h00	26%
1114-2009-2*	Workshop	9h00	11%
115-2009-1*	Workshop	8h30	15%
1115-2009-2*	Workshop	8h30	16%
1204-2009	Workshop	2h30	32%
1205-2009	Workshop	10h30	30%
1206-2009	Workshop	9h14	40%
0629-2010	Workshop	3h30	80%
0512-2010	Conference	1h30	36%

- measurements taken with 2 sensors of different construction in parallel

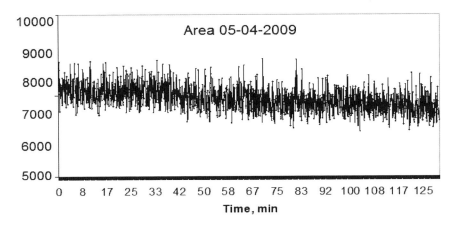

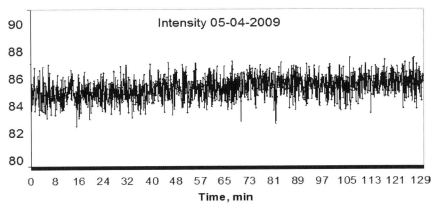

Fig. 6.32. Changes of parameters in control experiments.

CLINICAL STUDIES OF THE INFLUENCE OF RECONNECTIVE HEALING

THE INFLUENCE OF THE RECONNECTIVE HEALING ON PSYCHO-PHYSIOLOGICAL STATE OF ATHLETES

ST PETERSBURG APRL 2011

The double blind test in accordance with CONSORT Protocol was carried out with 20 apparently healthy volunteers - athletes of high level - of the different gender and age for the evaluation of the potential of body energy, stress level and physical endurance in control group and in the experimental group under the influence of Reconnective Healing.

The athletes were measured before and after intensive physical loading (10 min functional capacity ergometric testing Tunturi EL-400) in initial condition and in a week after:

Reconnective Healing in experimental group;

in conditions of normal functioning in control group.

GOALS OF THE STUDY

Assess the effect of the Reconnective Healing upon vegetative regulation of the heart rhythm, basing on the data of variation of pulse measurement (rhythmo-cardiography), energy reserve parameters, the recovery of hemodynamic parameters after a functional capacity ergometric testing and the blood analyses.

TEST PARAMETER BEING USED

1. Heart Rate Variability HRV.
2. Blood Pressure.
3. Pulse rate.
4. Maximal O2 uptake (VO2 max).
5. Energy profile (EPC/GDV parameters).
6. Blood parameters (clinical and biochemical).

PARTICIPANTS

20 apparently healthy volunteers – athletes of high level – members of the Russian national teams.

Age 17.6 +/- 1 year.

16 men and 4 women.

All participants are living in the School of Olympic Reserve, so they have the same type of life, same food, and same living conditions.

Testing was done 24 hours after the last training and 12 hours after the last meal.

All participants were divided to two groups in random order.

Informational Consensus Form with every participant was signed where the terms of the experiment were explained.

PROCEDURE OF THE TEST

Tests were performed in two sessions.

Test 1

Every person was measured in the following regime.

1. All parameters of the person measured (background 1).

2. Functional capacity ergometric testing for 10 min (cycle ergometer Bike General Electric Healthcare by General Electric Co). Testing done in steps: 1st step 100 Wt loading with 60-65 rounds per minute, every 2 min loading increased by 50 Wt. Blood pressure measured every 2 min.

Physical loading standards are as follows:

Submaximal pulse for every person in accordance with WHO recommendations:

Pulse = $0.85 * (220 -$ age in years)

PWC170 = W x 170 - rest pulse /pulse load - rest pulse VO2 max = 2.2 x PWC 170 + 1070 (maximum oxygen intake).

3. All parameters measured just after loading (after test 1).

4. Participants of the experimental group have the Reconnective Healing, was performed by Eric Pearl and Instructor.

5. Participants of the control group were in the conditions of normal functioning.

Test 2 in a week after the Test 1.

Procedure is the same as in the Test 1.

TECHNIQUE

The following instruments have been used in the study:

1. GDV instrument produced by KTI Co, Russia (www.ktispb.ru).

2. HRV "Cardio-meter - MT» "Mycard-Lana" Co.

3. Stress system "General Electric Healthcare Cardiosoft" with the cycle ergometry "Bike General Electric Healthcare" (General Electric USA).

4. Blood test initially and after a week with the biochemical analyzer KFK-3 and the haematological analyzer "Celly 70" with reagents of the "Vital-diagnostics" Co.

Blood was taken from the elbow vein in the morning before the food intake. Parameters measured were as follows:

complete blood count, total protein, urea, total cholesterol, total bilirubin, AST, ALT, CPK, creatinine, glucose, lactate. After loading study was conducted: CPK, and lactate.

DATA PROCESSING

Data were processed in "GDV SciLab" and "MS Excel" programs. Statistical significant difference when $p < 0.05$

EXPERIMENTAL RESULTS

ELECTROPHOTONIC (GDV) ANALYSIS
DATA PROCESSING

For every participant four sessions were measured:

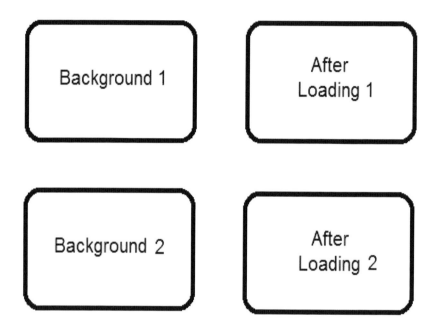

Fig.7.1. Experimental sessions.

In every session 10 fingers of every person was measured in two modes: with and without a special film, applied to the electrode of the GDV instrument. 20 images for every person were processed in the "GDV SciLab" and "GDV Diagram" programs and 17 parameters were calculated for every finger – all-in-all 170 parameters for every person. Statistical analysis and cross-correlations of data using Student t-test was done in MS Excel program.

RESULTS OF THE ELECTROPHOTONIC STUDY

IMMEDIATE INFLUENCE OF THE RECONNECTIVE HEALING SESSION

People from the experimental group had two sessions of the Reconnective Healing. Two of them had two sessions in different days. They were measured with GDV before and after the session. Results are presented in a Table and figures. As we see from the presented data, for most of participants sessions had fast positive effect.

As we see from the data, immediately after the Reconnection Healing session about half of participants had their energy parameters increased, while in a week after the session this effect became statistically significant. This signifies the importance of the study of time dynamics of the Reconnection Healing effects.

Table 7.1. Number and %% of participants having different effects immediately after the Reconnective Healing session.

	Increase	Constant	Decrease
Area Emotional	7	1	4
%%	0.58	0.08	0.33
Area Somatic	8	1	3
%%	0.67	0.08	0.25
Intensity Emotional	7	1	4
%%	0.58	0.08	0.33
Intensity Somatic	8	1	3
%%	0.67	0.08	0.25
Entropy Emotional	5	1	6
%%	0.42	0.08	0.50
Entropy Somatic	6	0	6
%%	0.50	0.00	0.50

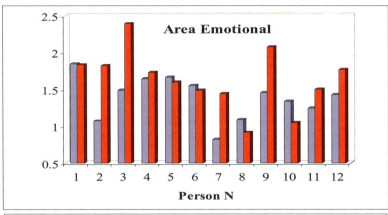
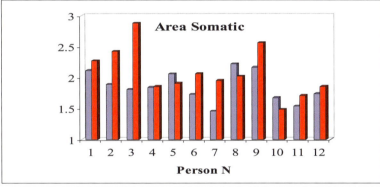
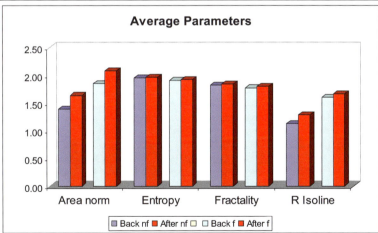

Fig.7.1. Changes of EPI parameters averaged for the experimental group initially and immediately after the Reconnection Healing session.

Science Confirms Reconnective Healing

Statistical Analysis of Data

Two sets of data are considered statistically different, when the result of t-test p < 0.05.

Test 1 - the first testing; Test 2 - testing a week later.

Table 7.2. Results of t-test for between-groups comparison.

	Test 1			
	Initial		After Load	
	Emotional	Somatic	Emotional	Somatic
Area norm	0.09	0.25	0.03	0.35
Intensity	0.92	0.14	0.00	0.05
Form Coef	0.97	0.10	0.00	0.19
R Isoline	0.23	0.07	0.00	0.34
R Circle	0.13	0.55	0.80	0.98
Noise %%	0.08	0.98	0.06	0.99
	Test 2			
	Initial		After Load	
	Emotional	Somatic	Emotional	Somatic
Area norm	0.53	0.00	0.00	0.01
Intensity	0.01	0.00	0.28	0.98
Form Coef	0.25	0.00	0.10	0.28
R Isoline	0.47	0.00	0.01	0.53
R Circle	0.84	0.00	0.19	0.00
Noise %%	0.29	0.00	0.03	0.00

As was demonstrated by the statistical analysis, in Test 1 in initial condition both in Emotional and Somatic States no statistical differences between experimental and control groups was found for most indexes, which shows that groups were equal both on emotional and somatic states. People were divided to experimental and control groups in a random order.

After a week – in a second test - statistically significant difference between experimental and control groups in initial condition and after loadings was found on several parameters both in Emotional and Somatic States.

These results may be presented in the graphic form (fig.7.2-7.3).

To evaluate the trend of the changes in experimental and control groups we may compare difference in parameters between background and after loading measurements. Results are presented in Tables 7.3-7.4 and at fig. 7.4-7.5.

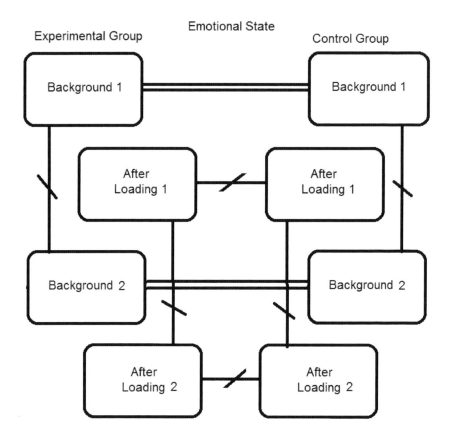

Fig.7.2. Statistical comparisons for the Emotional State.
=== no statistical difference; --/-- statistically significant difference.

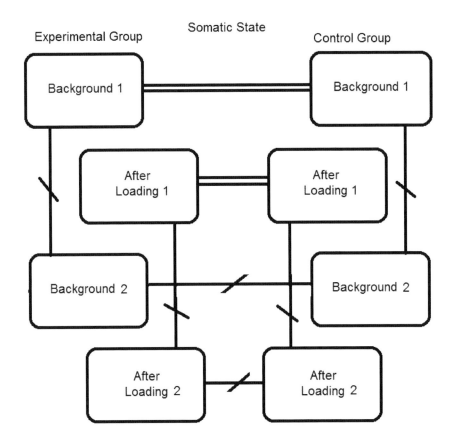

Fig.7.3. Statistical comparisons for the Somatic State.
=== no statistical difference; --/-- statistically significant difference.

Science Confirms Reconnective Healing

Table 7.3. T-test comparison between reactions

Difference between initial and after load measurements in Experimental and Control groups in Test 1 (initial).

Emotional response.

	Experimental group (1)	Control group (2)	t-test
Area norm	0.48	0.36	0.02
Intensity	0.89	0.60	0.01
Form Coef	5.20	3.05	0.00
Entropy	0.18	0.16	0.01
R Isoline	3.88	2.39	0.00
L Isoline	1.40	1.20	0.20
Noise %%	1.60	1.10	0.00

Somatic response

	Experimental group (1)	Control group (2)	t-test
Area norm	0.29	0.30	0.87
Intensity	2.92	2.50	0.67
Form Coef	0.78	0.69	0.34
Entropy	0.13	0.13	1
R Isoline	1.37	1.13	0.87
L Isoline	6.00	4.70	0.003
Noise %%	4.40	3.40	0.005

1 - Exp_Backgr_1_ - Exp_Load_1_

2 - Contr_Backgr_1_ - Contr_Load_1_

Table 7.4. T-test comparison between reactions

Difference between initial and after load measurements in Experimental and Control groups in Test 2 (A week after).

Emotional response.

	Experimental group (1)	Control group (2)	t-test
Area norm	0.28	0.48	0.00
Intensity	5.36	8.58	0.00
Form Coef	3.91	6.57	0.00
Entropy	0.18	0.30	0.00
R Isoline	2.63	3.96	0.00
L Isoline	1.38	2.00	0.02
Noise %%	0.70	1.30	0.00

Somatic response

	Experimental group (1)	Control group (2)	t-test
Area norm	0.26	0.28	0.65
Intensity	3.07	4.29	0.05
Form Coef	1.31	1.73	0.10
Entropy	0.13	0.14	0.85
R Isoline	1.50	1.65	0.54
L Isoline	0.70	0.90	0.09
Noise %%	0.68	1.00	0.00

1 - Exp_Backgr_2_ - Exp_ Load _2_

2 - Contr_Backgr_2_ - Contr_ Load _2_

Science Confirms Reconnective Healing

INITIAL TEST 1

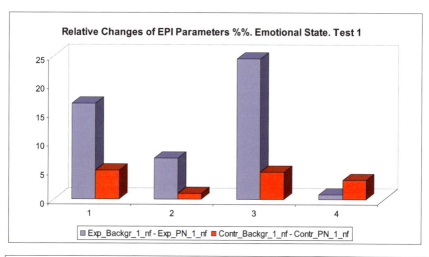

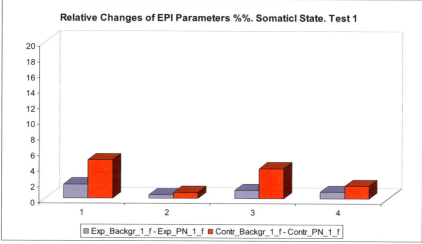

Fig.7.4. Difference in relative parameters between background and after loading measurements in experimental and control groups in the first test.

As we see from the graphs in the initial test response to the loading in experimental group was less adequate (difference is bigger) compared with control group, although this difference was not statistically significant for most of parameters.

TEST 2 . AFTER A WEEK

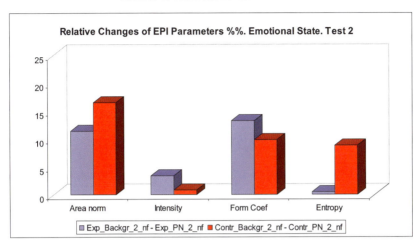

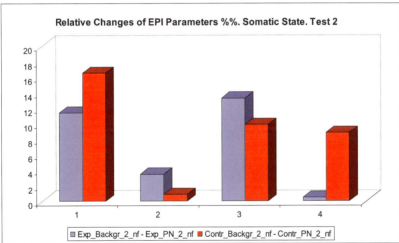

Fig.7.5. Difference in relative parameters between background and after loading measurements in experimental and control groups in the second test.

As we see from the graphs, after a week in a second test reaction to loading of the experimental group was much better compared with a control group. For most parameters the difference was statistically significant.

RESULTS OF THE EVALUATION OF THE CARDIOVASCULAR SYSTEM ACTIVITY

List of acronyms:

BP – Blood Pressure

ALRS – Activity Level of the Regulatory Systems

CVS – Cardio Vascular System

EP – Energy Pendant

EPC – Electrophotonic Camera

GDV – Gas Discharge Visualization

VBI – vegetative Balance Index (AMO/dX)

VRI – vegetative Rhythm Index (AMO/MO×dX)

PARP – activity of regulatory systems (AMo/Mo)

SI – stress Index of the regulatory systems (AMo/2ΔX×Mo)

PARS – activity of regulatory systems, is a generalized characteristic of rhythmogram

RESULTS OF THE STUDY

EXPERIMENTAL GROUP

Table 7.5. HRV Data in the Test 1 and Test 2 for the experimental group

Indexes	Test 1		Test 2		t-test	F-test
	Aver	St.D	Aver	St.Dev		
Rest						
Blood Pressure systol. (mmHg)	122,2	12,3	112,8*	14,2	0,012	0,682
Blood Pressure diastol. (mmHg)	73,4	10,0	71,0	8,5	0,311	0,647
HR (beats/min)	55,1	6,7	57,2	9,9	0,242	0,269
HRV indexes Initial						
NN., ms	1074,3	108,9	1054,9	199,7	0,398	0,090
Мо, ms	1050,0	105,4	1038,9	208,8	0,457	0,057
АМо, %	30,6	9,2	32,2	10,1	0,260	0,786
RRmin., ms	876,4	87,0	892,9*	185,5	0,256	0,036
RRmax., ms	1248,4	132,2	1202,7	203,9	0,232	0,219
dX, ms	372,0	120,4	309,8*	71,0	0,027	0,152
CV, %	6,5	2,1	6,0	1,9	0,084	0,721
SDNN, ms	70,2	23,4	62,7	20,0	0,064	0,673
RMSSD, ms	76,3	22,5	65,2	22,2	0,113	0,978
NN50count	103,0	36,1	93,3	36,4	0,292	0,974
pNN50, %	49,0	16,2	45,8	17,9	0,360	0,767
MD, ms	61,8	17,3	53,3	18,4	0,133	0,859
VBI	107,2	96,6	115,7	65,1	0,356	0,280
VRI	3,1	1,8	3,5	1,3	0,256	0,381
PARP	29,3	10,3	32,6	15,1	0,245	0,278
SI (Baevsky)	52,6	51,6	60,1	43,0	0,334	0,617
PARS	5,3	1,5	3,8*	2,0	0,024	0,367
HF, ms^2	1519,9	888,5	1406,6	1170,5	0,262	0,428
LF, ms^2	1562,2	1084,0	890,6*	551,2	0,014	0,070

Science Confirms Reconnective Healing

VLF, ms²	1189,2	1280,2	1033,3	1008,8	0,173	0,513
Summ, ms²	4271,3	2675,5	3330,4*	2293,2	0,046	0,675
LF/HF	1,1	0,6	0,9	0,8	0,313	0,627
LF, %	47,1	17,2	43,2	16,4	0,259	0,902
HF, %	52,9	17,2	56,8	16,4	0,259	0,902
HRV indexes after loading						
RRav., ms	787,4	81,1	761,9	65,7	0,158	0,563
Мо, ms	760,0	73,8	733,3	66,1	0,131	0,768
Амо, %	47,3	17,3	49,7	15,1	0,187	0,702
RRmin., ms	696,8	57,1	676,4	45,7	0,137	0,540
RRmax., ms	902,8	130,7	892,9	113,4	0,171	0,7
dX, ms	206,0	93,6	216,4	80,9	0,467	0,691
CV, %	5,2	2,3	5,1	1,6	0,260	0,299
SDNN, ms	42,0	21,3	39,4	13,8	0,203	0,240
RMSSD, ms	33,9	23,5	29,3	15,2	0,167	0,238
NN50count	32,5	37,1	26,3	24,8	0,159	0,299
pNN50, %	15,9	18,1	11,4	12,0	0,152	0,266
MD, ms	26,8	17,8	22,6	11,9	0,139	0,270
VBI	345,0	327,0	316,4	305,7	0,410	0,860
VRI	8,7	6,5	6,4*	2,8	0.289	0,039
PARS	63,6	27,0	69,4	29,6	0,172	0,787
TI SI (Baevsky)	241,7	248,6	233,6	261,0	0,381	0,880
PARS	4,2	2,8	3,4	2,8	0,443	0,983
HF, ms²	970,7	1288,6	591,2*	605,9	0,133	0,045
LF, ms²	574,8	666,8	508,2	437,4	0,297	0,249
VLF, ms²	341,7	258,9	349,4	176,3	0,401	0,293
Total ms²	1887,2	2003,1	1448,9*	903,3	0,151	0,035
LF/HF	1,7	2,2	1,8	1,5	0,060	0,276
LF, %	49,4	21,6	53,9	23,9	0,075	0,763

HF, %	50,6	21,6	46,1	23,9	0,075	0,763
Time of the heart rhythm relaxation	11,5	4,8	11,8	2,5	0,319	0,076
Time of the blood pressure relaxation	6,0	3,1	5,3**	1,1	0,197	0,009
After loading						
Blood Pressure systol (mmHg)	197,8	26,3	186,0*	26,5	0,029	0,968
Blood Pressure diastol. (mmHg)	87,1	23,6	86,3	28,3	0,428	0,593
Total (1/min)	171,7	2,2	171,7	1,0	0,443	0,055
VO2 max (ml/min/kg)	54,5	5,2	53,2	7,4	0,146	0,301

*- p<0,05; **- p<0,01

As we see from the Table 5, in the Test 2 against the Test 1 of experimental group a set of statistically significant changes of parameters was found.

Arterial pressure decreased statistically significant at rest from 122.2 to 112.8 mm Hg; after loading from 197.8 to 186.0 mm. Hg. PARS at rest decreased from 5.3 to 3.8 units. After loading VRI, HF, and time of the restoration of a blood pressure had significant decreased during experiment.

These changes indicate on economization functions of cardiovascular system in rest and its mobilization at a load with the least physiological cost. It demonstrate to the intensifying of adaptation CVS.

Science Confirms Reconnective Healing

Table 7.6. Data of blood analysis for the experimental group

	Test 1		Test 2		
	Aver	St.Dev.	Aver	St.Dev.	t-test
Hb	154.9	10.1	158.3	12.5	0.518
RBC 1012/L	5.2	0.4	5.2	0.4	0.892
HCT	45.2	3.5	44.1	3.0	0.441
WBC 10^9/L	6.2	1.7	5.9	1.0	0.693
IMM %	1.5	1.5	1.8	1.1	0.655
Neutrophils %	50.2	8.6	58.4	4.4	0.020*
Eosinocytes %	2.2	1.8	3.3	2.0	0.205
Basophiles %	0.8	0.9	0.2	0.4	0.105
Lymphocytes. %	35.9	9.3	28.6	5.0	0.050*
Monocytes %	9.4	2.1	8.8	1.6	0.488
ESR mm	6.1	3.1	5.2	2.1	0.483
O. albumine. moll/L	74.4	3.2	74.8	2.2	0.725
Urea. mol/L	6.3	1.2	5.4	0.7	0.050*
Cholesterol. mol/L	4.9	0.8	4.6	0.5	0.383
Bilirubin. mol/L	22.0	10.3	18.1	8.4	0.381
AST mol/L	20.0	3.6	20.0	4.3	1.000
ALT mol/L	34.5	10.2	25.3	11.9	0.085
Creatinine	105.7	24.5	98.7	15.3	0.477
Glucose moll/L	5.6	0.6	5.2	0.4	0.124
CPK before	108.7	29.0	94.7	13.4	0.202
CPK after	163.9	24.3	158.6	12.6	0.562
Lactate before loading. mol/L	2.0	0.5	1.9	0.4	0.802
Lactate after loading. mol/L	8.2	1.5	8.5	1.1	0.711

*- p<0,05;

As we see from Table 6, in experimental group significant positive changes of blood parameters in a week after the Reconnective Healing were found. These changes indicate significant positive shift in the body metabolism, in particular, increase of reaction to loading, faster restoration after the loading and decrease of the level of endogen intoxication together with the increase of non-specific immunity. These changes were found for most of participants (see fig. 7.5). In the control group no changes in blood indexes were found.

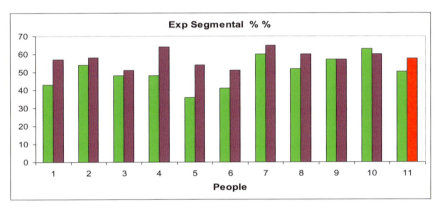

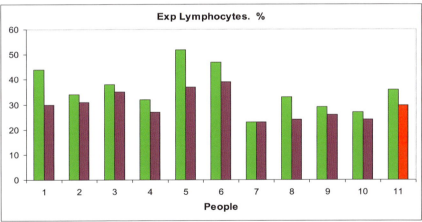

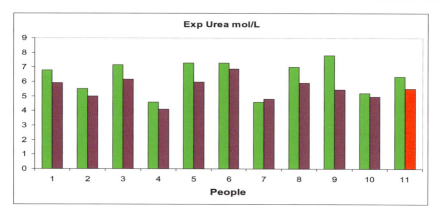

Fig.7.5. Blood parameters for individual participants initially and after a week (11 - average on the group).

CONTROL GROUP

Table 7.7. Indexes of the HRV in the Test 1 and Test 2 for the control group

Indexes	Test 1		Test 2		t-test	F-test
	Aver	St. Dev	Average	St. Dev		
Rest						
Art Pressure syst (mmHg)	110,5	14,1	105,5	10,3	0,146	0,369
Art Pressure dias (mmHg)	73,1	9,0	70,9	11,1	0,328	0,545
Pulse (1/min)	70,0	12,3	61,8	9,8	0,080	0,512
HRV indexes Initial						
RRav., ms	912,2	204,6	968,1	146,0	0,243	0,329
Mo, ms	885,0	216,1	945,0	172,3	0,321	0,511
Амо, %	31,9	8,8	30,7	13,2	0,779	0,247
RRmin., ms	734,4	185,8	773,6	123,4	0,217	0,238
RRmax., ms	1098,4	206,9	1153,6	191,5	0,331	0,821
dX, ms	364,0	68,8	380,0*	176,6	0,752	0,010

Science Confirms Reconnective Healing

CV, %	7,9	2,4	7,7	3,9	0,912	0,157
SDNN, ms	69,4	18,9	76,9*	43,9	0,590	0,019
RMSSD, ms	63,9	21,4	81,4**	46,7	0,231	0,029
NN50count	73,7	34,2	91,1	45,8	0,174	0,400
pNN50, %	36,1	16,9	44,7	22,5	0,176	0,409
MD, ms	48,6	19,2	66,2	37,0	0,117	0,064
VBR	92,4	35,8	132,5**	163,6	0,409	0,001
VRI	3,4	0,9	6,4**	7,6	0,250	0,001
PARP	37,8	14,0	34,7	20,2	0,647	0,291
TI	55,3	25,2	80,7**	112,0	0,452	0,001
PARS	3,9	1,7	4,8	1,9	0,279	0,728
HF, ms^2	1357,5	1037,6	1642,9	1604,0	0,514	0,210
LF, ms^2	1610,0	1603,2	2196,5*	3421,5	0,631	0,034
VLF, ms^2	1219,3	836,9	1980,6**	2614,3	0,322	0,002
Summ, ms^2	4189,8	3046,4	4838,6*	7504,2	0,790	0,013
LF/HF	1,7	1,7	1,5	1,2	0,746	0,278
LF, %	54,4	17,7	53,6	13,5	0,922	0,432
HF, %	45,6	17,7	46,1	13,4	0,951	0,416
HRV indexes after loading						
RRav., ms	696,8	84,8	722,1	60,0	0,340	0,318
Mo, ms	665,0	85,1	700,0	66,7	0,242	0,477
Амо, %	60,2	12,2	53,0	19,9	0,229	0,161
RRmin., ms	634,8	75,4	641,2**	28,8	0,775	0,008
RRmax., ms	785,2	112,9	847,6	100,3	0,187	0,730
dX, ms	150,4	45,7	206,4	86,0	0,078	0,074
CV, %	3,9	0,6	4,8**	1,8	0,115	0,005
SDNN, ms	27,3	7,9	35,1	14,9	0,119	0,074
RMSSD, ms	21,2	16,4	23,6	12,5	0,690	0,423
NN50count	13,3	33,5	13,0	16,8	0,981	0,051

pNN50, %	6,5	16,4	6,3*	8,1	0,974	0,048
MD, ms	17,3	14,3	17,7	8,9	0,931	0,167
VBR	451,9	217,6	392,9*	489,3	0,688	0,024
VRI	11,2	4,0	9,3	7,6	0,419	0,073
PARS	92,6	25,6	78,4	37,9	0,190	0,256
TI	354,1	184,1	303,5*	415,0	0,681	0,024
PARS	5,4	2,0	3,9*	2,2	0,038	0,748
HF, ms^2	150,9	141,4	190,3	211,8	0,594	0,244
LF, ms^2	287,5	158,2	358,9	277,0	0,459	0,111
VLF, ms^2	202,5	105,7	452,1**	415,0	0,103	0,001
Summ, ms^2	640,9	281,8	1001,3*	723,4	0,144	0,010
LF/HF	3,3	3,6	2,7	1,9	0,349	0,079
LF, %	68,7	13,1	68,0	12,2	0,751	0,827
HF, %	31,3	13,1	32,0	12,2	0,751	0,827
Time of the heart rhythm relaxation	14,9	4,3	11,5*	3,7	0,024	0,665
Time of the arterial pressure relaxation	4,6	1,5	6,6*	1,4	0,039	0,880
After loading						
Art Pressure syst (mmHg)	178,9	27,1	179,5	25,9	0,948	0,896
Art Pressure dias (mmHg)	90,2	13,7	86,6	21,2	0,609	0,211
Pulse (1/min)	171,5	6,3	171,6	3,7	0,915	0,125
MOI (ml/min/kg)	49,9	6,5	51,2	8,8	0,224	0,393

*- $p<0,05$; **- $p<0,01$

As we see from the Table 7.7 in the control group the change of several parameters denote relative decrease of functional activity and a reaction to the loading in the Test 2 compared with the Test 1 against experimental group.

Table 7.8. Data of blood analysis for the control group

	Test 1		Test 2		
	Aver	St.Dev	Aver	St.Dev	t-test
Hb	151.7	10.5	151.8	10.8	0.984
RBC 1012/L	5.3	0.5	5.2	0.4	0.616
HCT	44.4	3.5	44.3	3.0	0.962
WBC 10^9/L	6.6	1.5	6.5	1.2	0.857
IMM %	0.5	1.1	1.1	1.1	0.234
Neutrophils %	52.0	11.9	55.9	10.9	0.454
Eosinocytes %	2.5	2.6	2.8	1.9	0.775
Basophiles %	0.7	0.8	0.6	0.5	0.749
Lymphocytes. %	34.6	10.5	30.4	8.4	0.338
Monocytes %	9.7	2.8	9.2	2.0	0.647
ESR mm	6.8	6.6	4.5	3.1	0.333
O. albumine. moll/L	78.3	2.0	78.2	2.9	0.965
Urea. mol/L	5.6	1.0	5.7	0.8	0.906
Cholesterol. mol/L	5.0	0.4	5.0	0.2	0.536
Bilirubin. mol/L	16.7	6.1	17.0	4.8	0.892
AST mol/L	19.1	2.9	19.6	2.3	0.677
ALT mol/L	21.5	7.8	20.6	7.0	0.787
Creatinine	103.5	10.4	104.9	11.0	0.777
Glucose moll/L	5.3	0.3	5.4	0.4	0.432
CPK before	105.8	30.1	97.8	22.7	0.511
CPK after	176.9	18.2	180.2	30.7	0.773
Lactate before loading. mol/L	2.1	0.2	2.1	0.2	0.548
Lactate after loading. mol/L	9.5	1.2	9.3	0.9	0.728

As we see from the Table 7.8, no significant changes in the blood parameters between initial and a week later measurements were found, while in the experimental group significant changes were found on 3 parameters.

CONCLUSIONS

1. In initial condition no difference was found between experimental and control groups which signifies that groups were randomly selected.

2. After a week – in a second test – statistically significant difference between experimental and control groups was found for several lot of tested parameters.

3. Reaction to loading in the experimental group in the second test was much better compared with a control group. For most parameters difference was statistically significant.

4. Energy parameters demonstrated statistically significant difference between experimental and control groups on several indexes which characterize the quality of the Energy Field.

5. After a week in experimental group was found significant decrease of a blood pressure in rest and a systolic pressure after loading.

6. Increase of the economization function in rest, the efficiency of the activity cardiovascular system in the loading, and also faster restoration of both functional and blood parameters after loading demonstrate to the intensifying of adaptation CVS.

7. The significant positive changes in blood parameters for the experimental group showed increase of metabolic, immune, antitoxic and antioxidant activity of the organism.

We may conclude that session of Reconnective Healing had statistically significant positive influence on the functional state, humoral activity, physical condition and reaction to loading for the group of yang athletes in a week after the influence. This signifies long-lasting effect of Reconnective Healing and its significance for well-being and preparation of athletes.

8. INFLUENCE OF RECONNECTIVE HEALING ON HUMAN IMMUNE STATUS AND PSYCHO-PHYSIOLOGICAL STATE

ST PETERSBURG JUNE 2011

The double blind test in accordance with CONSORT Protocol was carried out with 40 apparently healthy volunteers of different age and gender for the evaluation of the immune status, body energy, psychological status and stress level in control group and in the experimental group under the influence of Reconnective Healing.

People were measured in initial condition and 7-10 days after with one session of Reconnective Healing in experimental group and in conditions of normal functioning in control group.

GOALS OF THE STUDY

Assess the effect of the Reconnective Healing upon vegetative regulation of the immune system status, psychological status and energy reserve parameters in experimental group compared with the control group.

TEST PARAMETER BEING USED

7. Immune status from blood parameters.
8. Energy profile (EPC/GDV parameters).
9. Psychology parameters

PARTICIPANTS

40 apparently healthy volunteers.

Age 33.5 +/- 11.0 years

11 men and 29 women.

All participants are living in Saint Petersburg, Russia.

All participants were divided to two groups in random order.

Informational Consensus Form with every participant was signed where the terms of the experiment were explained.

PROCEDURE OF THE TEST

Tests were performed in two sessions.

Test 1

Every person was measured in the following regime:

In the morning before the meal blood from the elbow vein was taken.

After this Electrophotonic imaging (EPI) test was made and participants filled psychological questionnaires (background).

On the same day in the experimental group was carried out one-time mental training with Reconnective Healing.

Test 2 in 10 days after the Test 1.

Same procedure as in Test 1.

TECHNIQUE

The following instruments have been used in the study:

GDV instrument produced by KTI Co, Russia (www.ktispb.ru).

Blood test initially and after 10 days with analysers of the immune status "Vital-diagnostics".

Blood was taken from the elbow vein in the morning before the food intake.

The immune status included determination of lymphocyte subpopulations with monoclonal antibodies (CD3, CD19, CD4, DR, CD8, CD56+16), determination of circulating immune complexes and immunoglobulins (IgA, IgG, Ig M).

Psychological status was examined by the test POMS (Mc Nair) with determing tensor (T) depression (D) aggression (A) vigorous (V) fatigue (F) confusion (C), the Luscher color test (total deviation (TD) and vegetative factor (VF).

DATA PROCESSING

Data were processed in "GDV SciLab" and "MS Excel" programs.

Difference was considered as statistical significant when $p < 0.05$.

Two people from the experimental group had to depart to business trip, so they experienced an oxidative stress and increased radiation during flying. They were excluded from the final analysis. Control group was decreased by two people as well.

EXPERIMENTAL RESULTS
IMMUNE STATUS
EXPERIMENTAL GROUP

Table 8.1. Date of the immune status in the Test 1 and Test 2 for the experimental group

Indexes	Test 1		Test 2		t-test
	Average	St.Dev	Average	St.Dev	
IgA (mg/dl)	245,50	102,98	237,59	100,02	0,083
IgG (mg/dl)	1179,17	283,94	1026,24*	340,59	0,045
IgM (mg/dl)	152,56	76,47	141,88	58,85	0,313
Immune complexes	78,32	42,84	65,84	35,63	0,141
CD3 (%)	65,26	6,89	69,88*	7,78	0,022
CD3 (count)	1282,44	298,31	1356,53*	304,46	0,035
CD19 (%)	10,67	4,42	10,74	4,33	0,470
CD19 (count)	208,44	92,25	208,18	101,90	0,318
CD4 (%)	38,98	7,90	42,58*	6,84	0,009
CD4 (count)	766,56	225,53	818,65*	177,25	0,025
DR (%)	4,94	3,27	4,97	3,66	0,361
DR (count)	92,89	62,24	98,00	78,93	0,352
CD8 (%)	24,99	8,07	27,38*	8,89	0,013
CD8 (count)	490,61	182,36	546,65*	235,51	0,014
CD 56+16 (%)	15,99	6,67	14,41	6,07	0,103
CD 56+16 (count)	320,00	165,14	284,41	146,58	0,289

*- p<0,05

As we see from the Table 1, in the Test 2 against the Test 1 in experimental group a set of statistically significant changes of cell parameters of immune system was found. Basic parameters increased statistically significant during experiment. Count of CD3 from 1282,44 to 1356,53; CD4 from 766,56 to 818,65; CD8 from 490,61 to 284,41 of cells (p<0,05) (see fig.1-4).

The dynamics of immunological parameters for the experimental group (cells)

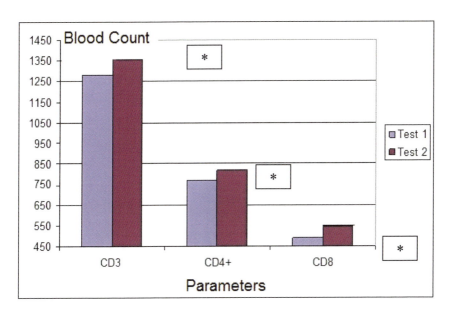

Fig.8.1. Averaged on experimental group blood parameters in Test 1 and Test 2.

These changes were found for most of participants (see fig. 8.2-4).

Science Confirms Reconnective Healing

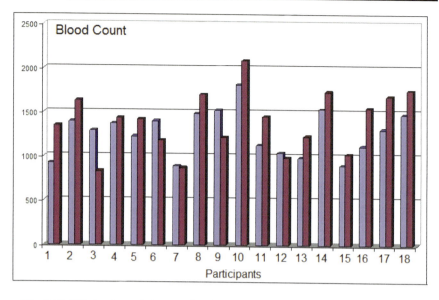

Fig.8.2. 72% of participants had an increase in CD 3 on the test 2.

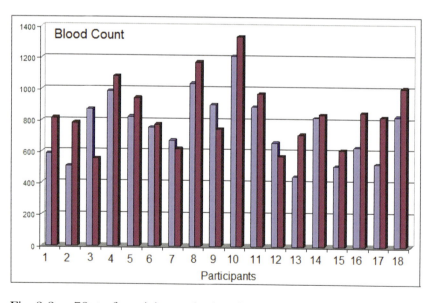

Fig. 8.3.   78% of participants had an increase in CD 4 on the test 2.

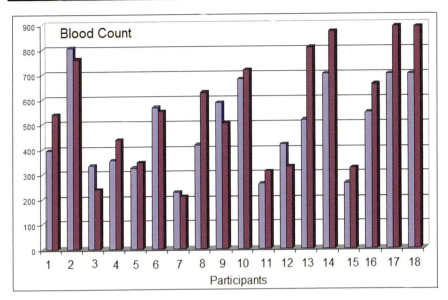

Fig. 8.4. 67% of participants had an increase in CD 8 on the test 2.

Parameters of humoral immunities are almost unchanged. No significant changes CD 19, IgA, IgM. And only IgG significant decreased from 1179,17±283,94 to 1026,24± 340,59 mg/dl (p<0,05).

These changes indicate significant positive shift in the immune system, in particular, growth of indicators total lymphocytes, helper and cytotoxic lymphocytes. This indicates the increase of non-specific immunity, adaptive capacity of the immune system, the control of the autoimmune processes and some decrease of the level of endogen intoxication.

Science Confirms Reconnective Healing

CONTROL GROUP

Opposite changes were observed in the control group (Table 2).

Table 8.2. Date of the immune system in the Test 1 and Test 2 for the control group

Indexes	Test 1		Test 2		t-test
	Average	St.Dev	Average	St.Dev	
IgA (mg/dl)	295,12	108,36	285,76	112,39	0,076
IgG (mg/dl)	1268,41	177,92	1162,76***	175,28	0,0001
IgM (mg/dl)	138,12	80,44	131,82	71,31	0,125
Immune complexes	64,66	53,38	62,04	40,05	0,0001
CD3 (%)	69,76	9,15	65,41*	11,04	0,046
CD3 (count)	1542,18	485,69	1289,24**	437,96	0,005
CD19 (%)	12,02	3,40	10,71*	3,13	0,034
CD19 (count)	257,35	99,92	202,94**	61,42	0,003
CD4 (%)	44,04	9,22	40,68	7,84	0,087
CD4 (count)	976,35	362,15	799,18*	270,11	0,012
DR (%)	4,61	2,95	3,98	2,17	0,073
DR (count)	95,18	70,67	76,53*	42,64	0,038
CD8 (%)	25,32	5,76	24,14	5,43	0,068
CD8 (count)	537,35	170,38	469,35*	165,90	0,013
CD 56+16 (%)	16,66	7,13	15,35	5,70	0,102
CD 56+16 (count)	370,24	168,52	303,00*	131,49	0,024

*- p<0,05; **-p<0,01; ***-p<0,001

As we can see from the data almost all parameters of immune system in the control group have decreased in comparison with experimental group in which improvement of the majority of indicators was marked.

In the Test 2 against the Test 1 in control group significant decreased the following parameters: CD3, CD19, CD4, DR+, CD8, CD 56+16 (Fig.8-5,6).

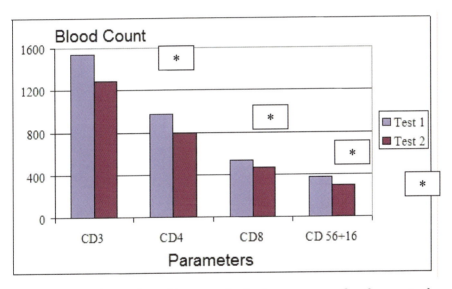

Fig.8.5. The dynamics of immunological parameters for the control group (cells CD3, CD4, CD8, CD 56+16) * P < 0.05.

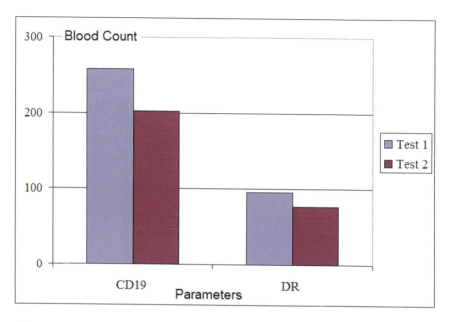

Fig. 8.6. The dynamics of immunological parameters for the control group (cells CD19, DR). *- p<0,05; **-p<0,01.

Parameters of humoral immunities are almost unchanged. Parameters CD 19, IgA, IgM and IgG significant decreased. These changes can be interpreted as stressful. This may be related to the situation that practically all participants were on the eve of the annual holidays after a year of stressful activity.

Science Confirms Reconnective Healing

ELECTROPHOTONIC (GDV) ANALYSIS

DATA PROCESSING

In every session 10 fingers of every person was measured in two modes: with and without a special film, applied to the electrode of the GDV instrument. 20 images for every person were processed in the "GDV SciLab" and "GDV Diagram" programs and 17 parameters were calculated for every finger – all-in-all 170 parameters for every person. Statistical analysis and cross-correlations of data using Student t-test was done in **MS Excel** program.

In the Test 1 in initial condition both in Emotional and Somatic States no statistical differences between experimental and control groups was found, which shows that groups were equal both on emotional and somatic states. People were divided to experimental and control groups in a random order.

For all parameters the following percentage of changes P%% was calculated :

$$P\%\% = (T2 - T1)/T1,$$

where T1 and T2 – the values of the parameter in the first and second tests, accordingly.

Tables 8.3. Results of statistical tests for different parameters for the Emotional State (no filter) and Somatic State (with filter)

Before/after	no filter T-TEST	no filter F-test	filter T-TEST	filter F-test
Area	0.002	0.455	0.000	0.885
Normalized area	0.111	0.030	0.010	0.473
Average intensity	0.006	0.000	0.000	0.083
Number of fragments	0.240	0.000	0.553	0.000
Shape factor	0.016	0.299	0.149	0.000
The entropy of the isolines	0.001	0.389	0.048	0.629
Fractality of the isolines	0.144	0.000	0.003	0.001
The average radius of the isoline	0.002	0.429	0.000	0.967
Sstandard deviation of the radius	0.039	0.441	0.010	0.000
The length of the isoline	0.315	0.028	0.830	0.010
Radius of the inscribed circle	0.184	0.265	0.001	0.793
Percentage of the internal noise	0.064	0.030	0.023	0.011

These results may be presented in the graphic form (fig.8.7).

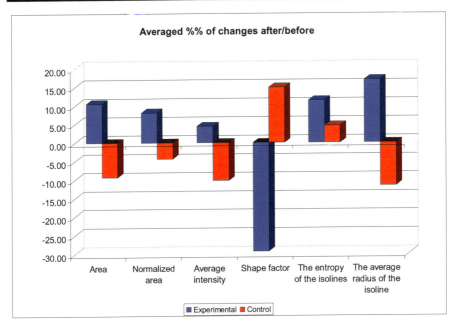

Fig.8.7. Averaged %% of changes after/before on different parameters for the experimental and control groups. All the difference are statistically significant.

As we see from the Table 8.3, in a second test - statistically significant difference between experimental and control groups was found on most parameters both in Emotional and Somatic States. Fig. 7 demonstrate, that in experimental group all changes were positive (decrease of Shape Factor signifies more balanced state), while in control group most of parameters demonstrated negative tendencies.

PSYCHOLOGICAL STATUS

Psychological status was examined by the test POMS (Mc Nair) with determining tensor (T), depression (D), aggression (A), vigorous (V), fatigue (F), confusion (C), the Luscher color test (total deviation (TD) and vegetative factor (VF)/ Table 8.4 demonstrate results of the study.

Experimental Group

Table 8.4. Date of the POMS test and M. Lusher color test.

Indexes	Test 1		Test 2		t-test
	Average	St.Dev	Average	St.Dev	
Tension (T)	44,09	7,56	39,86	7,73	0,004
Depression (D)	43,45	8,77	40,95	6,65	0,030
Aggression (A)	45,64	10,80	41,50	6,49	0,035
Vigor (V)	51,45	6,93	53,00	7,42	0,185
Fatigue (F)	43,50	6,79	40,59	6,66	0,036
Confusion (C)	41,45	7,71	38,23	6,60	0,029
Total deviation (TD)	13,5	8,1	11,5*	5,8	0,01
Vegetative factor (VF)	1,5	0,5	1,5	0,5	0,5

*- p<0,05; **-p<0,01

We can see that all negative parameters of psychological status in experimental group have declined significantly. Vigor has increased, at least for some people. So the profile of POMS became more favorable after the experiment (Fig.8.8-8.9).

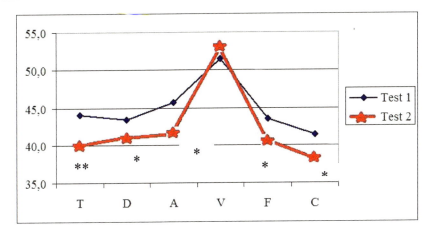

*- p<0,05; **-p<0,01

Fig.8.8. Date of the POMS test in the experimental group.

The Luscher test was conducted initially (Test 1) immediately after the Reconnective Healing (Test 2), and after 10 days (Test 3). Fig.8.9 shows the dynamics of the test.

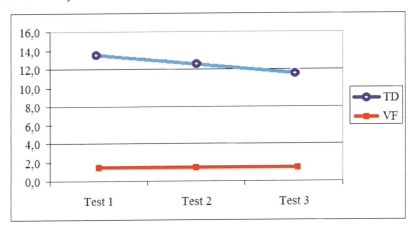

*- p<0,05

Fig.8.9. Date of the Luscher test in the experimental group

These changes indicate significant decrease of TD parameter, which reflects the positive impact on the psychological status of the participants.

CONTROL GROUP

Table 8.5. Date of the POMS test and M. Lusher color test.

Indexes	Test 1		Test 2		t-test
	Average	St.Dev	Average	St.Dev	
Tension (T)	42,5	7,2	40,9	6,8	0,070
Depression (D)	41,1	4,4	40,8	4,7	0,315
Aggression (A)	42,7	4,9	42,9	4,6	0,414
Vigor (V)	53,85	12,3	50,1	11,5	0,051
Fatigue (F)	41,05	6,6	42,1	7,1	0,197
Confusion (C)	39,45	5,7	39,1	6,0	0,290
Total deviation (TD)	14,1	7,2	12,1	7,2	0,155
Vegetative factor (VF)	1,4	0,5	1,4	0,5	0,239

As well as immunologic parameters psychological status in the control group had no significant changes. At the same time vigor decreased and fatigue increased (Fig. 8.10).

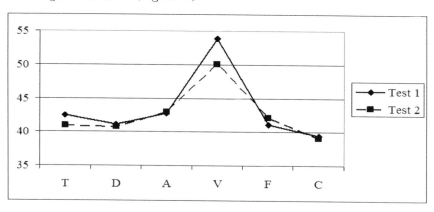

Fig.8.10. Date of the test POMS in the control group.

CONCLUSIONS

Significant changes in psychological and immune parameters under the influence of a single impact of Reconnective Healing on a group of 20 people prove the effectiveness of this intervention.

The following significant changes in the immune system have been identified: the general increase of lymphocytes, of the helper cells, and of the suppressor cells. Psychological status of the experimental group demonstrated significant improvement: negative psychological indicators reduced - tensor, depression, aggression, fatigue and confusion as well as the total deviation in the Lusher test.

Energy parameters demonstrated statistically significant difference between experimental and control groups on several indexes which characterize the quality of the Energy Field.

These changes prove multiple positive effects of one session of Reconnective Healing on deep mechanism of immune regulation, psyhomodulation (increase the mental power and decrease stress manifestations) and increase the immune response.

Apparently the impact affects the immune system through psycho-immune mechanisms. As a result, there have been significant positive changes in basic cellular subpopulations of the immune system.

No changes were found in the control group of 20 people.

We may conclude that one session of the Reconnective Healing had statistically significant positive influence on the immune system, body energy and psychological status for the group of people in 10 days after the influence. This signifies long-lasting effect of the Reconnective Healing and its significance for well-being of people.

Science Confirms Reconnective Healing

9. RECONNECTIVE HEALING WATER STUDY

Several experiments were conducted with the influence of the Reconnective Healing to water.

Experiment 1.
Procedure:

1. (5) bottles of Arrow Head, a commercial drinking water was placed in the 4 corners of the room & the 5th was by the table adjoining the podium, which was placed in the middle of room from where Instructor would be conveying to the attendees. Bottle classification: C1, C2, C3, C4, & S5.

2. Room layout: Chairs for seating 100+, arranged as an arc, podium in middle & massage tables on the other side of podium.

3. (5) Control bottles for study was placed behind the front desk of the resort.

Purpose of Study: To observe at the response of each days events from all the stations where the bottles were positioned.

C1-By research table;

C2 -MTB corner;

C3 - Next MTB corner;

C4 - RC info + educational corner;

S5 - Stage/Podium table.

Science Confirms Reconnective Healing

Data Capturing sequence: All data capturing was done at the end of each days session from C1-C4 & S5. Data was captured with EPC/GDV Pro instrument using a standard water-testing process with syringe in a dynamic mode with 30 frames/per second and 5 sec duration.

Observations:

Day 1

C1 had very strong variations of a signal;

C2 had very strong variations of a signal;

C3 had very strong variations of a signal;

C4 had no data;

S5 quite stable signal;

Day 2

C1 had very strong variations of a signal;

C2 had very strong variations of a signal;

C3 had no response;

C4 quite stable signal;

S5 had very strong variations of a signal.

The control bottles had no signal response.

Experimental graphs of GDV Area variations are presented below.

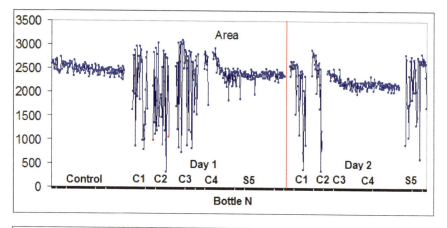
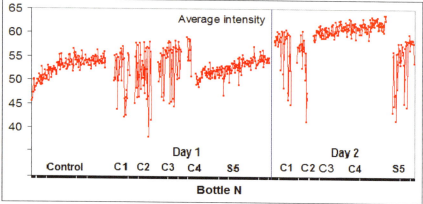

Fig. 9.1 Reconnective Healing water experiment

Experiment 2

Procedure:

Commercial bottled water (Arrow Head) was used for this study.

1. Each participant would have a 10 min RCH session on a bottle & data was captured with EPC Pro in a dynamic mode.

8 participants whose initials are indicated are: D; J;; K; P; R; SA; and S participated in the experiment.

Results:

As we see from the graphs, participants D, J, K, and S produced significant effects on water.

As people are 70% liquids, this gives us idea of the mechanism of influence to people.

Remarks: This is a pilot study initiated by Instructor to observe if there are measurable patterns that can be observed.

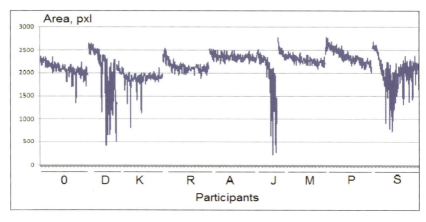

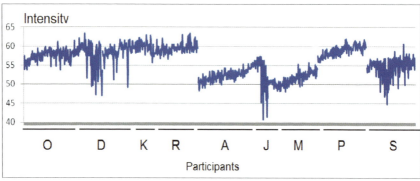

Fig.9.2. Reconnective Healing water experiment

Experiment 3

Procedure:

Experiments were conducted wit the influence of Eric Pearl to the "Sputnik" sensor and to water measured with GDV. Commercial bottled water was used for this study.

Results:

In all cases the influence was statistically significant (see figures).

Fig. 9.3 Statistical processing of Water Sensor data under the Reconnective Healing influence with Area and Intensity parameters.
1 – background; 2– influence.

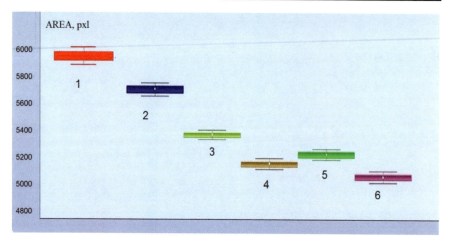

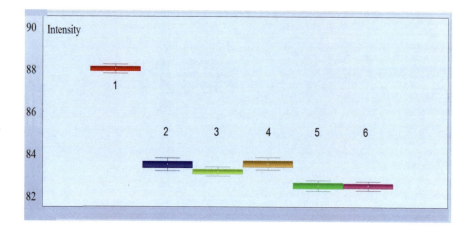

Fig.9.4. Statistical processing of "Sputnik" sensor data under the Reconnective Healing influence with Area and Intensity parameters.

1 – background; 2-6 – different modes of influence.

DISCUSSION

In all cases of water study we may see statistically significant reaction of water to the process of Reconnective Healing.

In the first mode bottles were standing in the seminar room for a day and influence was lasting for a long time. At the same time we see that not all the water responded to the influence. This fact and comparing with a control water having no changes indicate that water have been structured under the influence of Reconnective Healing process. We may assume that structurization of space has non-uniform character in the room.

This type of experiments should be repeated.

Significant structurization of water took place under the influence of directed Reconnective Healing by the trainers. Effect was different for different people which may be related to different modalities of their influence.

10. CONCLUSIONS

We have observed experimental data collected during 14 months with different instruments, by different researchers, and in different parts of the world. All these data are quite consistent and have very similar type of variations. They all suggest that in the process of Reconnective Healing structurization of space in the auditorium takes place.

People may have different response to this process, and this response may take long time. We expect that Reconnective Healing starts harmonization of the energetic processes in the body, and depending on initial conditions this process may take different time and have different outcome. Long-term observations of participant's conditions with collecting data on the Quality of Life and wide spectrum of physiological parameters would be strongly recommended.

Sensor data undoubtedly demonstrate that Reconnective Healing have strong positive environmental effects which may be expected extend much broader than the range of the auditorium. It is important to compare effects of Reconnective Healing by individuals or by a group of experienced people.

Water experiments demonstrated that water changes its properties under the influence of Reconnective Healing both in the case of directed attention and with bottles standing in the room. Control experiments had no effects at all. We keep in mind that human body is 70-80 % water, so it may tell us about mechanisms of Reconnective Healing influence to the body physiology.

More experiments should be conducted to support presented suggestions.

Research was organized and conducted by the following persons:

Konstantin Korotkov, PhD, Professor.

Elena Gavrilova, PhD, MD, Professor.

Oleg Churganov, PhD, MD, Professor.

Oleg Shelkov, PhD, Professor.

Anna Korotkova, PhD.

Dmitrii Orlov

Krishna Madappa

Lucy Robertson

REFERENCES

[i] Korotkov K., Korotkin D. Concentration dependence of gas discharge around drops of inorganic electrolytes. J of Applied Physics, 2001, 89, 9, 4732-4737.

[ii] Korotkov K. Human Energy Field: Study with GDV Bioelectrography. Fair Lawn, NJ: Backbone Publishing Co. 2002

[iii] Korotkov K. Aura and Consciousness: New Stage of Scientific Understanding. St. Petersburg, Russia: State Editing and Publishing Unit "Kultura". 1998.

[iv] Korotkov K., Williams B., Wisneski L. Biophysical Energy Transfer Mechanisms in Living Systems: The Basis of Life Processes. J of Alternative and Complementary Medicine, 2004 10, 1, 49-57.

[v] Polushin J, Levshankov A, Shirokov D, Korotkov K. Monitoring Energy Levels during treatment with GDV Technique. J of Science of Healing Outcome.. 2:5. 5-15, 2009

[vi] Rgeusskaja G.V., Listopadov U.I. Medical Technology of Electrophotonics – Gas Discharge Visualization - in Evaluation of Cognitive Functions. J of Science of Healing Outcome. V.2, N 5, pp.15-17, 2009

[vii] Owens J, Van De Castle R: Gas discharge visualization (GDV) technique; in Korotkov K (ed): Measuring Energy Fields State of the Science. Fair Lawn, NJ, Backbone, 2004, pp 11-22.

[viii] Bundzen P. V., Korotkov K. G., Korotkova A. K., Mukhin V. A., and Priyatkin N. S. Psychophysiological Correlates of Athletic Success in Athletes Training for the Olympics Human Physiology, Vol. 31, No. 3, 2005, pp. 316-323.

[ix] Bell I., et.al. Gas Discharge Visualisation Evaluation of Ultramolecular Doses of Homeopathic Medicines Under Blinded, Controlled Conditions. J of Alternative and Complementary Medicine, 2003, 9, 1: 25-37

[x] Korotkov K., Krizhanovsky E., Borisova M., Hayes M., Matravers P., Momoh K.S., Peterson P., Shiozawa K., and Vainshelboim A. The Research of the Time Dynamics of the Gas Discharge Around Drops of Liquids. J of Applied Physics. 2004, v. 95, N 7, pp. 3334-3338.

[xi] Vainshelboim A.L., Hayes M.T., Momoh K.S. *Bioelectrographic Testing of Mineral Samples: A Comparison of Techniques.* Journal of Alternative and Complementary Medicine. 2005: Vol. 11, No. 2, pp. 299-304.

[xii] Measuring Energy Fields: State of the Art. GDV Bioelectrography series. Vol. I. Korotkov K. (Ed.). Backbone Publishing Co. Fair Lawn, USA, 2004. 270 p.

[xiii] Korotkov K.G., Matravers P, Orlov D.V., Williams B.O. Application of Electrophoton Capture (EPC) Analysis Based on Gas Discharge Visualization (GDV) Technique in Medicine: A Systematic Review. The Journal of Alternative and Complementary Medicine. January 2010, 16(1): 13-25.

[xiv] Korotkov K, Orlov D, Madappa K. New Approach for Remote Detection of Human Emotions. Subtle Energies & Energy Medicine • V 19, N 3, pp 1- 15, 2009